Moving On

and other Zimbabwean stories

Moving On

and other Zimbabwean stories

edited by
Jane Morris

'amaBooks

ISBN 978-0-7974-8879-3
EAN 9780797488793

© This collection: amaBooks, 2017

© Each contribution remains the copyright of the author

Published by amaBooks
P.O. Box AC1066, Ascot, Bulawayo
amabooksbyo@gmail.com
www.amabooksbyo.com

Cover Design: Veena Bhana

Cover Art: *Untitled II* by Thakor Patel

amaBooks would like to express their thanks to the Beit Trust for
making this publication possible, and to Bongani Kona, Murenga
Joseph Chikowero, Ignatius Mabasa, Thabisani Ndlovu, Cliford Zulu
and the National Gallery of Zimbabwe in Bulawayo for their assistance.

Contents

The Silt Path

Togara Muzanenhamo

When the old man woke into the darkness of that winter morning, it was with a heaviness and fatigue that tested his strength. All night he had dreamt of the calf and slept uneasily. In the windowless room he had lived in for most of his adult life, he did not strike a match but simply rolled the blankets up off the floor, packed sweet potatoes he had boiled two days ago, then slipped his feet into broken boots that he secured around his ankles with baling twine. He licked his fingers and removed dry parcels of caked sleep from the corners of his eyes. Stepping out of the hut, he was met with the smell of wood smoke and the ringing of cooking pots. Darkness had just begun peeling back off the horizon, stars to the west still nailed bright to the black canvas above.

There was little morning talk in the compound, men woke and dressed silently, ate silently – walked out in gangs to the work yards, sheds and silos. They walked with only a few words between them until they were stationed at their posts, breath cupped warm in their hands. But his silence was different. It was an enduring bitterness held back in his throat by this life that had shown him nothing but labour, this land that had given him nothing to own, where death had taken those he loved, discarding them over the ridge to the great beyond, their graves unmarked.

Adjusting the thick coat he slept in, he walked along with the others – labourers, drivers, graders, mechanics – raising a shallow cloud of grey dust off the powdered clinker path that leads to a broad thoroughfare lined with giant gum trees. The men's silhouettes grew

1

starker as the stars faded, deep stains of diesel and engine oils mapped across their overalls.

In his mind he had planned his route to seek out the calf, walked the land in his dreams, the images of his journey set in a simple sequence: the blue triangular dam that hugged the border of the estate, the wide open jaws of the stone quarry, the solitary windmill in the west.

By the time the sun rose, he was completely alone, walking away from the distant roar of engine and machine, away from fields still bright with maize stover – he was far into the lower arm of the estate, his boots wet with dew thawed from frost. The air cleared as he emerged from untamed bush to a wide pleated strip of harrowed earth. Along the fireguard a row of wood poles shrunk into the distance with staves of barbed wire glistening with the music of the sun. As he approached the most easterly border of the estate, the smell of water thickened the air with the weight of growth and vegetation. He scaled the muscled bank of the dam and saw the sky off the water's surface, a sky cradled by bulrushes bowing into carpets of soft silver moss. He took off his coat and trailed through the grass, his bamboo cane slipping through the dry undergrowth that fell away from the dam's soggy banks.

He would find nothing, no newborn or carcass.

*

Sitting on an anthill, he rests and eats. The noon sun overhead, his buttocks flat on his shadow. As he sits there, he thinks of the calf's mother wandering back to the pens after two days of being lost – casually strolling in at dusk, alone. For months he had seen the heifer's indifference to its own pregnant state, noticed the cow's gradual dislocation from the herd – the separate task of its ways lead by a solitary glare mirrored in his own distant eyes. So when he lead the heifer into the maternity pen and watched the cow lay down and curl its head to take its own teat, he knew the beast was damned. And without question, or the need of any summons, he knew that the next morning he would have to walk out in search of the calf, the search bringing him here to where he now sits – his pale nut-brown skin absorbing the winter sun.

The dirt road snakes away from the dam for three miles, the bush heavy on either side. Flat-top and umbrella acacia spaced out far and wide. As he walks, the rhythm of his steps crunch and sweep monotonously, his left foot scuffing the ground. Over the years he has watched his shadow thin out to a crippled stain, his gait collapse from its fluent stride to a heavy limp that angles and drags his body forward. How long can he go on this way, he thinks, alone with a body willing him to stop, a heart worn out.

Born on the estate to a cold, reticent mother, it was clear to him from an early age that he was not like the other boys – boys who, when roughed-up and white with dust from the fields, were bathed by mothers, their wet naked skin shining like dark polished soapstone. His skin retained the hue of the sand, the blond satin dusk that slipped off the others' heels. His mother had never married, nor did she ever speak of his father, but from the very beginning everything about his features could be traced back to the master of the homestead: the loose curl of his hair, the deep cleft chin, his cool grey eyes. And yet, even with his lineage, he knows he is merely a product of the place, held within its boundaries with a lifelong bond that will have him die here. And after his death, his body will be carted away to a field not too far from the windmill where his mother, wife and children lie.

He thinks of the labourers working on the estate now, the men and women who surround him – theirs is a simpler deal, they have come from somewhere else, know the world beyond the dam and boundary fences, have their own villages, have seen the towns and – perhaps – maybe even the city. Some even know how to read.

The dirt road gently curves then dramatically ascends to a broad jagged shelf overlooking a deep bare crater – a wound in the earth a tenth of an acre wide. Here, he does not whistle or call but stands and stares down into the burrowed hole – neither wishful nor expectant, neither wanting nor refusing what he may or may not find. He stares into the quarry searching its depth. It has been almost fifty years since gravel was last carted for railway ballast, yet the pit has not been secured, an iron trailer ripped by rust lies upturned on the opposite side from him. The sweet putrid smell of death rises from naked shadows where the pit comes to an end. Leaning over, he follows the stench with his nose and spots a large antelope, the fine brown pelt collapsed on the scaffolding of bone, the head beginning to malt, the animal's temple waxy and bald. Apart from that, there is nothing that will draw him in further.

Crossing back into the grasslands he heads west for an hour before entering a vast treeless paddock, the sun falling cool and flat over a red sea of knee-high grass, which rolls in slow silent waves.

In the distance he can see where the field dips into a shallow valley, where a thin scar of naked earth snakes up to the ridge he is heading for. As he walks, his shadow stretches out ahead of him, slipping in and out of the darkening grass, till the grass thins and opens up revealing a meandering belt of sand. In no time the cool breeze falls thick and settles above the soft ground. He wades through the cooling depths of air hugging his shins, the full moon about to rise behind him. He has walked this path, known its course, ever since he was a boy, the dried up riverbed sucking in his heels, the pale sifted sand infiltrating his boots with the cold deliverance of silt.

He knows the calf will not live through another night. Even if it rests sheltered in the grass, he knows the late evening air will whisper with winds that mark the land white with streaks of frost. The silt bed will take him up to the old windmill standing tall on the ridge, the wind-pump's metal sails turning slowly above a quiet concrete water trough. It is here he believes the calf's mother may have given birth. But for now he stops, turns and gives his back to the sun – looks down across the field, scans the pastures for any sign of disturbance; and as he stares down and across – he sees how far he has come, the homestead and compound knitted tight into a distant snatch of green, the feeding pens and cattle race almost out of sight, the slaughterhouse swallowed up by the land.

He knows time is running out and imagines the calf curled somewhere in the field, head to hoof in a fragile pose new to its delicate life. Perhaps, not too far from the windmill's trough, he'll hear a weak nasal low – the call coming from somewhere hidden where shadows of growth lurch over the calf like a protective wing or steady arm. Even as young as the calf is, the old man knows no living thing wants to die out in the open, exposed to wind, rain or sun. Perhaps the calf is already dead. He doesn't know. Would it be better if it survived, confined to these fields, knowing nothing but the paddocks, the pens, the plunge dip that soaks the beasts' hides with heavy phosphate salts? He doesn't know. But walking the cold silt bed, he knows the calf's mother will be culled – the self-milking brood cow first fattened before being sent to the slaughterhouse.

Standing alone – an empty feeling blossoms in his chest then wastes away. The cold air falls dry on his skin, his body locked between the shifting balance of the rising moon and setting sun. In the distance, silos and outhouses of the estate slowly fold into the fading features of the landscape, the homestead's electric light shimmering like a clutch of fallen stars. All he has known fades out before him. Drawing in a deep breath, he turns away and walks up to the ridge. The windmill's silhouette gradually falls into a darkness that will eventually be replaced by moonlight.

What's in a Name?

Mzana Mthimkhulu

Even before my foot hit the ground as I got out of the car, I yelled to all in the house, 'Come and join me on the veranda.'

With the puppy pressed to my chest, I slammed the car door and hurried up the veranda steps. I sat down on a garden chair and my wife marched in, her niece Nomhle close behind.

'This better be fast,' she said. I gestured to her to sit down but she shook her head. 'Some of us are busy. We have to finish preparing supper before load-shedding hits us.'

Ndabezinhle, our gardener, tiptoed onto the veranda. As though preparing to sit on eggs, he slowly lowered himself on to a chair.

My two children Njabulo and Lwandle dragged their feet in and slumped on chairs. Both sipped soft drinks as they continued to look through the window so as not to miss a second of the high school musical they had been watching on television.

Suddenly noticing the puppy under my chair, Njabulo wrenched his eyes away from the window, exclaiming, 'A new puppy!' He knelt beside the chair and playfully poked the puppy. Saliva dripping from its gaping jaws, the puppy growled and bared its fangs. Njabulo pulled back his hand.

Lwandle's eyes widened. 'A police dog in our home?'

I smiled and once again congratulated myself on the purchase. This cross breed between a ridgeback and a basenji was a delight to watch. Here was a dog with the ferocity required to guard my family and property in these troubled times.

'Ladies and gentlemen,' I addressed my family, 'we are gathered to choose a name for the puppy. This is important. We must all

6

participate.' I paced the cement floor before continuing. 'After considering several names, it has been decided the dog's name will be Ndevueziqamulamankomitsho.'

'What?' Njabulo exclaimed as he spluttered the drink on his shirt and almost choked. His eyes pleaded with me. 'That will be the end of my social life. What will my friends make of me coming from a family whose dog has such a long name?'

I snorted. 'What social life can a fourteen-year-old have?'

'The name is unpronounceable,' Lwandle said.

I patiently explained, 'Real African names always have meaning. To capture the full meaning, sometimes the names are long. As for being unpronounceable, no person on earth should ever find sounds from her own language difficult to pronounce. There is not a single foreign sound in the name and so it cannot be unpronounceable for a Ndebele speaking family.'

'What then is the meaning?' Lwandle asked.

'Good question,' I said. Suddenly I felt as though I was in a lecture room with knowledge-hungry students looking up to me.

'Ndevueziqamulamankomitsho was a guerrilla. The oppressive white regime labelled him a terrorist but peasants saw him as a freedom fighter. The so-called security forces feared him as much as ordinary people loved him. The man robbed white-owned ranches, shot game and gave his loot to hungry peasants. He was a modern day Robin Hood. As the name suggests, his beard was so long and bushy that more than half of the cup disappeared into it when he was drinking.

'Names live up to what they are based on. Just as his people loved Ndevueziqamulamankomitsho and colonialists hated him, the dog will be adored by its family but strike terror in the hearts of intruders. As a bonus, the name is a reminder of the armed struggle we successfully waged against colonialists.'

'You are right Dad,' Njabulo nodded.

'Baba, not Dad,' I corrected him. 'I may be progressive but would be conceding too much if I allowed my children to address me by a foreign word.'

'Sorry, Baba,' Njabulo said. 'I agree a name must have meaning.'

'That's my boy.' I nodded. 'Offspring of the lion clan. A true Sibanda. You have roared like the lion you are. Magnificent jaw that pulverised the elephant's thigh bone.'

'Thank you Baba.' Njabulo smiled, enjoying his clan praises. 'I have thought of a wonderful name for the puppy. Look at its body, light brown like dry savannah grass, but its feet, white as refined mealie-meal. The feet look like its socks. I therefore name it Socks.'

'Well done son, that is a name with meaning,' my wife exclaimed. 'The matter is settled.' She turned to leave.

I barely controlled my fury. 'A foreign name in my house? No way!'

'Huh,' my wife grunted. 'Thanks to people like Ndevueziqamulamankomitsho, we now live in a democratic country. Let us settle this with a vote. Voting—'

'No need to preach about democracy,' I said. 'I played a leading role in the struggle to liberate this country.'

'Good,' my wife nodded. 'All those for the name Socks, hands up.' Five hands shot up.

She glanced at me with a triumphant grin. 'Assuming you will bother to vote, it is five against one. Ladies and gentlemen, by popular vote, the dog will be called Socks.' She swung round and left. Nomhle followed her. I glared at Ndabezinhle and he also left. Njabulo and Lwandle stood up to leave but I stopped them.

'Listen,' I said. 'This is Africa. We practise democracy *our* way.'

Njabulo frowned. 'How?'

'We synchronise our voting with the African way of life.'

'Meaning?'

'Son, age in Africa is important. For each year one has lived, he or she becomes wiser. In African democracy, we should say one year, one vote. This is fair. No sexism. No tribalism. No racism. No regionalism. Daily, everyone gets older and wiser. Our voting must therefore give weight to the wisdom that comes with age.'

'That is alright,' Njabulo shrugged. 'Let us add the years of all five who voted for the name Socks and—'

'I am not yet finished,' I said. 'This is a Sibanda home. That *garden boy* Ndabezinhle is a Maseko, not a Sibanda. He therefore has no right to vote here.'

Njabulo shook his head in disbelief. 'Baba, Ndabezinhle has lived with us for ten years. How then—'

'I am not saying he must never vote,' I explained. 'Let him go and vote at the Maseko home, not here.'

'Okay,' Njabulo shrugged again. 'Ndabezinhle is disqualified but we still have mum's and Nomhle's votes. Mum is forty and Nomhle–'

'I was coming to that,' I said. 'Your mother and Nomhle are Ncubes, so they have no vote at the Sibanda home. They will vote at their Ncube home. Here, we–'

'But Baba,' Lwandle gaped, 'at Sunday school, they taught us that when a man and woman marry, they are no longer two, but one. Mother and you are one.'

'Sunday school?' I frowned.

'Yes, Sunday school,' Lwandle emphasized. 'And you are always telling us to obey Sunday school rules.'

'Aah…,' I chuckled. 'Yes… well… you see… you are taking this out of context. You cannot read just one verse and then claim to understand the Bible.'

'The verse,' she pressed on, 'goes on to say what God has joined together, let no man separate.'

I sighed and sat down. 'Actually… you see children… in life we need not quote the Bible only. Our African tradition has a treasure of wisdom we should draw on. One of our people's sayings goes; the one who has hurt herself is not cried for; it is the one who is hurt by another who deserves our sympathy. Your mother and cousin brought this upon themselves. They denied themselves votes by storming out before the election was over. They ran off before the re-run and cannot now cry foul.'

Njabulo shook his head. 'They left because the election was over.'

'But,' Lwandle said, 'they had to cook for all of us before the electricity goes.'

'Mum's and Nomhle's votes will not count here,' I said. 'Even the English have a saying about this: out of sight, out of–'

'But surely Baba–'

'My boy, only on television do children interrupt their parents in mid-sentence. Television – an electronic device that makes the young know more about faraway celebrities than their own origins – will not dictate how we do things! As I was saying – out of sight, out of mind. The Ncubes are out of sight and therefore have no vote here. Now, let us recount the valid votes. I am fifty-five years old – that gives me fifty-five votes.'

'Come Lwandle,' Njabulo said, standing up and extending a hand to his sister. 'The election ended when Mama left.' Hand in hand, the two started walking out.

'You will hear this before you leave,' I shouted. 'Njabulo, you are fourteen and Lwandle is eleven – that gives the two of you twenty-five votes against my fifty-five. So lady and gentleman, by popular vote, the puppy will be called Ndevueziqamulamankomitsho. Better luck when we vote again in five years.'

The following day I registered the puppy at the vet's as Ndevueziqamulamankomitsho.

But this was not an end to it. My family conspired against this progressive move. They never called the puppy by the name the family had voted for in a free and fair election. Even the neighbours and my children's friends chose to use the illegal, meaningless name. In no time, the puppy only responded to the foreign name of Socks.

To add insult to injury, the puppy never lived up to its early promise of being fierce and aggressive. Smothered by hugs, shampoos, kisses and three meals a day, it grew into a fat, lazy and disobedient pet that made friends with all and sundry. With a name like that, what else would you expect?

10

Moving On

Bryony Rheam

David was standing by the sink, dishcloth in one hand, dinner plate in the other, when Angela said, 'Dad, I want to come with you.' And then, as if to clarify matters, 'To Granddad's funeral. I want to come.'

He hadn't answered immediately, taking time to let the words sink in, pulling in his lips a little, watching his hand making slow circles on the plate with the cloth, as though it were not attached to him at all; as though it were someone else's hand, someone else's life.

She leaned against the kitchen counter, eyeing him with a wary concern. About a year ago, she had decided to shroud herself in black from head to toe, the only bit of colour remaining being the blue of her eyes. The dark eye makeup he found unsettling rather than intimidating, for it suggested a sadness not commensurate with her age and out of kilter with her body, which was young still, thin and angular and inhabited yet by that awkwardness particular to teenagers which, combined with a natural shyness, made her stoop slightly.

In the last year or so, she had become a living ghost, an entity who left the house without saying goodbye and entered it without him knowing. Her bedroom door was always closed, but, unlike other rooms occupied by teenagers from which loud music emitted or from where raucous laughter and insidious giggling slid through the tiny gap between door and carpet, hers was quiet. More than quiet; still. More than once, he had stopped and listened, just for something, anything: a creak of the bed, the soft sound of a pencil being put down on the desk, a cupboard door closing; a sign of life.

A stage, Nancy had said on the only occasion they had ever discussed their daughter's behaviour. It was early one morning in the

11

kitchen and she had been in a hurry putting on her earrings and dialling Marc from the office at the same time. 'It's just girls,' she began. 'Yes, I'll hold. I was like that.' Then she stopped to check herself in the mirror and run a fingertip around her lips to remove any excess lipstick. She pushed back her hair and then fluffed it up at the sides and did that funny shoulder roll that signified she was ready to leave.

'Marc, hi...' She grabbed her handbag and her laptop and made for the door. 'I should be there in five minutes. Listen, I've got some great ideas.' Then, as though she too were a ghost – or was it him that didn't exist? – she had gone.

There was a time when she would have blown a kiss to him and a time before that when she would have planted her lips on his cheek. 'Have a great day,' she would have said, ruffling his hair. 'I'll call you at lunchtime.'

David turned back to his daughter, who had shifted her gaze away from him and was attempting to assume the attitude of bored nonchalance that usually occupied her being. She wasn't quite successful for it was a look edged with a sense of disquiet, of waiting. It was the most impatient he had seen her. Aware of him watching her, she proceeded to channel this restlessness away from herself by taking a sip of water from a long glass then looking down at her nails, which were bitten to the quick and covered in black nail polish. She rolled two thin black plastic bangles up her wrist revealing a small tattoo of a rose, which he had not noticed being there before.

'Yes,' he said, placing the dinner plate on top of another one and reaching for a bundle of knives and forks. 'OK, yes. You can come. But you do know where it is, don't you?'

She put down the glass with a roll of her eyes.

'Africa?' He noticed a tongue stud. That was new too, wasn't it? Or was it? How long was it since they had last talked?

'Zimbabwe.'

She shrugged and nodded her head and then looked away from him. The cockiness had gone, replaced by a look of sad uncertainty. Zimbabwe was his territory, the subject on which no one, not Nancy, not Angela, could trespass. It rarely surfaced in conversation now and, if it did, it only elicited a bored response of silence or the occasional grunt in agreement or disagreement or the stock, automatic refrains of 'oh dear' and 'that's not good'.

Nancy wouldn't come to the funeral, he knew. There had been no suggestion of it when he told her of the phone call. She had been trying on a new dress in the full length mirror in her bedroom and the announcement seemed something of an irritation. She had paused in the middle of an action, one hand pressing down the front of the dress the other on her hip, and gave him a look as though to say he could have chosen a better time and not stolen her moment quite so completely. Then she carried on, one hand moving to her stomach, the other to the small of her back.

'Oh dear. When?'

'Last night. In hospital.'

'How?'

'Heart failure.'

'Yes, well. He has had a couple of scares before, hasn't he?' There was a sense of inevitability in her voice, as though something had come to its natural conclusion and nothing was to be done about it. She leaned forward close to the mirror and tweaked an errant hair in her eyebrow. Then, noticing a wrinkle at the corner of her eye, pulled her face into an odd taut smile that momentarily straightened out any lines.

'Yes,' he said, turning away. Her life, the dress, the occasion on which she would wear it, seemed little to do with him.

Later, as they sat silently eating the bolognaise he had made, he reading his book, she some financial report, she had looked across at him with a twinge of guilt and squeezed his hand. He withdrew his and turned a page.

'I'm going,' he said, without looking up. 'To the funeral.'

'Which is?' The hardness returned to her eyes, which narrowed slightly as she watched him.

'Tuesday.'

'Tuesday? But today is only–'

'Thursday.'

'Yes, Thursday. We're going away for the weekend, remember? We've had it booked for months.'

He paused while he fought the desire to tell her that *she* had had it booked for months and that he didn't want to go anyway, funeral or no funeral. He didn't like her so-called friends who were really just the people from the office; the way they talked business over breakfast and excused themselves to answer what were always urgent phone calls, making out that they didn't want to disturb the conversation but doing just that anyway by pacing up and down, phones in hand, rubbing their foreheads and rocking back on their expensive heels as though the fate of the world depended on them, so that all eyes followed them, waiting for their return and the inevitable words: 'Whew! Close call. If you'll excuse me, I need to do some work before lunch.'

He wanted to tell her that people didn't generally choose when to die. That they don't ask to have a look at diaries and memorise appointments so they can choose a quiet moment whilst no one is doing anything in which to slip away. He wanted to remind her that his father had died and that a little more sympathy may be in order.

Instead he said, 'I've booked the flight. I leave on Saturday.'

Perhaps out of some vague sense of respect or an awareness that she had not quite responded appropriately to his loss, she remained quiet, pushing a small pile of spaghetti to the side of the plate and marooning it there before putting her knife and fork together.

It annoyed him, the way she left the pasta. She had served herself hardly any in the first place as though again what she did take was out of some sense of misguided deference to his loss, but she couldn't carry the action through in its entirety and now heaped it on the side of the plate.

She took a sip of wine. 'I see.' She dabbed the corners of her mouth with a napkin and seemed to be waiting for him to say something. Apologise, maybe, but he didn't.

When the plan to take Angela with him was announced, the last of Nancy's sympathy for him evaporated.

'She won't go,' she retorted.

'She was the one who asked.'

Nancy was about to say something, but stopped and drew the words back in, snapping her mouth shut over them.

He obviously wasn't worth arguing with and the next moment she was in Angela's bedroom, the door firmly shut. He stood in the passage, listening hard and was briefly reminded of the times when Angela was a little girl and how he used to read her to sleep and then creep quietly away, shutting the door behind him and then stopping a moment to listen in case she had woken up.

14

Those were the days when Nancy didn't work and he went to an office every day. He had treasured those moments with Angela then, sitting on her bed and reading her his favourite childhood classics, watching as her eyes became heavy with sleep and she stuck her thumb in her mouth and cuddled up to her teddy.

It was to Angela that he had first told his Reg Browning tales. Fluent in isiNdebele, Reg was a boy who grew up in the bush in Africa, spending his days hunting and fishing. He was always tanned brown by the sun and knew how to make fire by rubbing two rocks together and how to carve whistles from pieces of wood with a pen knife. Indeed, Reg Browning lived in a timeless age in which politics played no part and there was no war or strife. It was when Angela had grown out of these stories that David had considered putting them to paper and so his first book had been published. Buoyed up by the success of the first adventure and the commission for subsequent novels, he and Nancy had decided that he would stay at home and write and she could resume her career.

He started as the door opened and Nancy emerged, thin-lipped and obviously annoyed. Seeing him, her mouth pulled to one side and she said in a very efficient school teacher fashion, 'Well, I have told her what to expect. Malaria and flies.'

'You don't get malaria in Bulawayo.'

She flicked his comment aside. 'And flies. And she'll have to boil the water no doubt and what's she going to do without electricity – well, that's her problem.' She looked at him down the length of her nose as though to suggest it was his problem as well.

'They do have electricity in Zimbabwe.'

'That's not what you said to me the other day when you were listing all the current woes your father was facing.'

He winced, but stayed calm. 'They might have power cuts but it's not as though they don't ever have electricity.'

Her look this time suggested he better check his facts.

'Look,' he said, wishing he didn't feel he was trying to placate her. 'It's a week, a week and a half at most.'

'A week and a half?'

He paused, looking at a white spot in the carpet half way between them where, in the phase before the goth phase, Angela had spilt blonde hair dye. It looked like an island in a deep green sea, a tiny island washed by emerald waves. 'I thought I might take her to Victoria Falls.' And then, somewhat superfluously by way of explanation, he added, 'She's never been.'

She stared at him before shaking her head and breathing out noisily. 'So, that's decided then.' She held his glance and then looked away. He walked back into the kitchen and made a list. Somewhere he felt a vague sense of triumph.

David lay in bed at the bed and breakfast in Bulawayo, thinking back on the last time he had seen his dad alive. It was three years ago and he had come to visit them in Brisbane. They had gone fishing on Peel Island and, although they did not catch much that day, what stayed with him was the sense of closeness he had felt to his father. He admired the man: the way he looked like a healthy sixty-five year old rather than eighty-three; the way he still managed to get around with ease and how he approached everything in life with a quiet optimism. At his father's core, David realised, was a great strength, a deep something which weathered every crisis. He didn't get annoyed or upset. His inner calmness buoyed him through the storms of life.

It annoyed Nancy, David knew that. Nancy thrived on deadlines and panic. Her day was a frantic emptying of the hour glass; for her, the sands of time seemed to run out more quickly, spurred on by an ever-enveloping feeling that there was never enough. He didn't realise until moments like this how much her frenetic approach to life had rubbed off on him. Like his dad, he stepped back from life, but unlike his dad, he watched it as a scared child might watch large waves come crashing in on the beach: frozen, afraid to run in either direction, hoping against hope that some outside force would bear him up and out of harm's way.

'Are you happy?'

'Yes,' he had said in response to his dad's question, although his reply was just that fraction of a second too slow to be considered an honest one. His dad had tilted his head sideways to look at him and let out his line a little more.

'That's good,' he said with a smile. 'I'm glad.'

David was reminded then of another time in his life when he was a child and he hadn't told the truth. Instead of castigating him, his dad had dropped to his haunches and put a hand on his shoulder.

16

'When you lie,' he had said, 'the only person you are trying to fool is yourself.'

David turned over in bed. It was a single for he had given the queen-sized bed to Angela. There was something comforting about the simplicity of a single bed. It reminded him of childhood, before life got complicated, before he got entangled in someone else's dreams. It reminded him of a time when, with a teenager's singularity of vision, he focused only on his life's purpose, when he lay on his back and dreamed of all the places he would go to, all the things he would do.

'How long have you lived in Australia?' the lady at the bed and breakfast had asked him as she had struggled to hold a large green and white umbrella and open the front door of the cottage at the same time. They had arrived the previous evening in the middle of a thunderstorm.

'Oh, about twenty years,' he had answered, but now as he lay in bed he realised it was much longer. Thirty-two.

'I hope you don't mind,' the lady had begun as she switched on the lights in the main bedroom, 'we have a dog.' She looked apologetic, as though the decision to keep the animal depended entirely on him. 'He's a lovely dog.' He watched the way she twisted the cottage key in her hands. 'That's yours,' she said, handing it over. 'He's just a bit big and bouncy. Doesn't know his own strength.' She gave a nervous shrug of her shoulders, a gesture which seemed at once an appeal for help and a resignation, as though the matter were entirely beyond her. And then, in an attempt at jollity: 'So are you here on a holiday?' She looked between him and Angela as though trying to work out the dynamics of the tired, lonely-looking pair.

'No,' he answered. 'My father died. We're here for the funeral.'

'Oh, I'm sorry.' She looked pained and her anxiety over the dog was momentarily forgotten.

'He was in a home,' he said, although he didn't know why for there was no need to explain. 'He was very fit for eighty-six, but he had a fall in the shower last July.'

'Last July?' she repeated and he knew what she was thinking. It took you all this time to come.

'He was in good hands,' he began. 'He was very well looked after.'

She looked away as though she had delved too deep. 'Well, I'll leave you to it. I am sure you're very tired. Good night.'

Now, as he lay watching a watery sun rise through the torrent of rain that still fell outside, he wondered at the honesty of his words. About a month after receiving the news of his father's accident, he had got an email from Anne, the sister of a friend from Bulawayo, asking him if he knew that his dad was on the most basic of medical aids, which was not covering the smallest of bills. Some of the expenses had been paid by an anonymous well-wisher and others by a donation from a charity for the elderly, but should he need further care, which was inevitable, was it at all possible for David to contribute?

The message had lodged like an arrow through his throat. He felt physical pain when he read the words. Over and over he read them; there was nothing accusatory about them, but he couldn't help feel a vague sense of criticism. He hadn't known; Dad had never said he was in need. Of course, David had bought his ticket when he came to visit and paid for everything while he stayed. But his needs had been minimal beyond the obvious ones of food and a place to stay. He never asked for anything, never seemed to want or need more than he had.

When Angela awoke, he made them tea. She didn't eat breakfast and he wasn't hungry. At eight, he and Angela went to the nursing home to collect his father's paperwork.

'Everything's ready to take,' the matron had pronounced in a bright, bustling manner as she unlocked the door to his room. She stood back to let them in, her eyes scanning Angela suspiciously. 'Take your time. We don't have anybody coming until Friday.'

David stood in the middle of the tiny room that his father had occupied and looked from the single bed pushed alongside one wall to the table in a corner on which stood a small bottle of Mazoe Orange, a glass and three old *Angler's Mail* magazines. On a shelf above the table was a photo of David's mother when she was in her early forties and one of David and Nancy with a very small Angela.

'Is this it?' Angela asked, looking around too. 'It's more like a jail cell.' Their eyes met and she looked away. 'Sorry,' she added, 'It's just... I'm sure it's very nice here.'

His dad's clothes were laid out on the bed and his drawers emptied. David ran his hand along the collar of a blue shirt, one of two, trying not to notice how the material was frayed and worn. He smoothed a crease out of a pair of trousers and then let his hand fall limp beside him.

'Look, Dad,' said Angela, who had pulled a child's painting from behind the family photo. It was one that she had painted at pre-school many years ago after one of her grandfather's visits. 'I remember doing this. He had just left and I missed him.' She held up the now-faded picture of a stick man with a large head and glasses and a large smile that took up most of his face. 'He kept this. All these years.'

David declined the matron's offer of a cup of tea, instead asking where his father's personal papers were.

'Oh, the undertaker's got those,' she stated, nodding her head.

'The undertaker? You mean the funeral has been arranged already?'

'Oh yes,' she nodded again. 'It's the standard one we offer here.' Service in the chapel followed by tea in the lounge.'

'And will he be buried or cremated?' David felt a hot flame of anger dart up his throat. He swallowed hard and took a deep breath.

'We're very lucky to have a plot allocated to us in the cemetery. Our board worked very hard to be given it.' She leaned forward in a conspiratorial manner. 'You don't want to be buried just *anywhere* in Bulawayo.' Another nod of the head.

'My father...' David began, then, feeling his throat contract, he stopped. 'My father always wanted to be cremated.'

'Well, unfortunately, the crematorium isn't working at the moment.' She raised her eyebrows meaningfully. 'But, luckily, we have this plot—'

'Yes,' David interrupted her. 'You said.'

That night after the funeral, Anne asked them to dinner. He had been a school friend of her brother, Peter, who now lived in Canada. Her eyes flickered over Angela in surprise, but she said nothing. David had warned his daughter that Zimbabwean society was still quite conventional and that they had probably no idea of goths in Bulawayo. Yet Anne's teenage son and daughter looked upon Angela with interest and immediately tried to engage her in conversation. Not immediately forthcoming in response, Angela had refused a glass of wine and opted for water instead. She pushed a small helping of chicken casserole round her plate, taking small, wary nibbles when she felt the need to show she was eating something.

The evening was a little stiff at first, especially after the first perfunctory remarks about politics and weather and who was doing what and where. Afraid of being drawn into the problems of everyday life in Zimbabwe, David had trod carefully on the edges of the conversation. They spoke about Brisbane and Australia and his writing.

'Your books do quite well, don't they?' Anne asked.

'Yes,' he answered. 'Apparently so.'

'I read a write-up once in a South African magazine.'

'Yes.' He tried to think of an appropriate rejoinder but words seemed to have escaped him.

Anne ate quietly, staring at her plate.

'So where do you get your ideas from?' she asked. 'It must take a lot of working out.'

David's heart sank. It was the stock question of inexperienced interviewers.

'Oh, here and there.'

She nodded. 'Quite amazing really.'

He looked sideways at her, not understanding the meaning of her remark.

'What I mean is, writing about Africa in the way you do and yet you haven't been here for years.'

The look he gave her this time was sharp and alert. He detected a prod behind the words, a hard dig.

'When, in fact, was the last time you were here?'

In the end, it was a relief when the coffee had been drunk and David could excuse them without rudeness.

The day after the funeral, David woke early. The rain had stopped and the day was brightening into a slow grey. He carried his running shoes to the door quietly and had a quick look into Angela's room. She lay sprawled on the bed, still clad in black, like a long thin spider. Her face was surprisingly clear of makeup though, her lips a natural pale pink. From this angle, she looked like Nancy, a much younger, relaxed Nancy, and David felt a momentary twinge, not for her, but for a time that seemed irrevocably gone. He pulled the family picture from his pocket and stared at it a full minute before putting it away.

He closed the front door behind him gently and walked down the long drive to the gate. As quiet as he thought he had been, the dog must have heard him and bounded closely behind him. It jumped up at him, landing its huge paws on his shoulders. He pushed it down and stroked its head, which it twisted upwards in a playful attempt to bite his hand. He unlocked the gate, opening it just enough to squeeze himself out. The dog pawed at the gate, but he managed to close it behind him.

'Good dog,' he said. 'Good dog.'

The dog whined and wagged its tail, waiting to be let out, but David ignored it and turned right onto the road. It was littered with potholes that had filled with rain water and the verges were thick with long green grass that was nearly as tall as he was. A lamppost leaned dangerously close to the ground. A couple of cars splashed through puddles or swerved recklessly to avoid them. A few people walked along: a schoolgirl holding her mother's hand, a maid in uniform, a man pushing a bike.

At the next junction, the road signs were missing, but he thought he knew where he was. The roadside was overgrown and the road itself dilapidated, but not much else had changed in the last thirty or so years. If he was right, their house was at the bottom of the road on the left.

On the back cover of each of his books was a short biography of David March. It read: 'Growing up in Rhodesia (now Zimbabwe), he spent his boyhood in the bush where he developed a love and knowledge of the outdoors.' In reality, he had grown up in town, in the leafy suburb of Hillside, but his publicist had insisted on changing the details to suit the readership. In fact, one interviewer had gone so far as to suggest he had grown up in a mud hut without electricity or running water and, although David had felt the lie had gone too far that time, it had almost certainly upped the sales of *Running Brave*, the third book in the series.

He stood outside the house; this was it. It must be. The basic wrought iron gate had been replaced by a huge black electric monstrosity and the hedge by a wall above which a bougainvillea stretched like a long pink feather boa. Unsure, he looked at the house next to it, which still had a fence through which he could see the garden and part of the house. He considered ringing the bell, but it was early still and he didn't want to wake anyone. Besides, he didn't want to have to explain. I used to live here. About twenty, no thirty, years ago. Australia. No, not a holiday. My father died. He was in a home.

He looked away. In the pocket of his shirt, he could feel the photograph rub against him.

Are you happy? Are you happy? He lives in Brisbane with his wife and daughter and their funny cat, Max. Are you happy? They enjoy taking walks together as a family and spending their weekends exploring south-east Queensland. You can lie to everyone, but you can't lie to yourself.

Are you happy?

Suddenly, David ran at the wall and tried to jump, but he fell back. He tried again, taking a longer run up this time, but again he failed. The third time, he stared hard at the wall before running with all his might, hands up, reaching, clawing for the top of the wall, which was rough and hard and cut his fingers. He leapt back in pain and lay sprawled on the wet grass, holding his hurt hand, squeezing back the tears.

'Dad? What on earth are you doing?'

It was Angela. In black, she was always in black. Always mourning – what? She looked as though she had been crying for streaks of black smudged across her face. Couldn't she go for a walk without metamorphosing beforehand?

'I'm just... going for a walk.'

'Looks like it,' she said, pulling him up.

He sat up, embarrassed that a tear had managed to escape, but she turned a blind eye.

'I was just looking for our house. We used to live – here, I think. Except we didn't have a wall or an electric gate.'

She looked up at the wall without much interest.

'How would anyone know what's behind that. You could have lived in any of these houses. They all look the same.'

'No they don't, Angela,' he snapped. 'They don't look the same!' It was the first time he had lost his temper with her for years. 'It's obvious,' he said, motioning to the wall with his outstretched hand, which was bleeding slightly. 'It's obvious that this house here is different to that house *there*.'

'Dad! You don't have to get so... so angry.'

'Don't I? Don't I?' He grabbed her by the shoulders and pushed her towards the wall of the garden. 'This was my house, this was my childhood, this is where *I grew up.*'

She looked wildly, blindly at the wall, pulling her shoulders together as though she were cold.

'Look, look! What do you see? Come on, tell me. *What do you see?*' He was shouting loudly now. A man and a woman stopped to look, then catching his eye, they walked on. He turned her round and round, his fingers digging into her shoulders, hurting her back.

She started to cry. 'I don't know, Dad. I don't know. I don't know what you want me to see.'

His hands dropped by his sides in exasperation and he was just about to launch another attack when a large dog bounded up and knocked him to the ground.

'You didn't close the gate,' he said, accusingly. He wiped a spot of blood off his forehead and rubbed his hand. 'You let the dog out.'

'I am sorry,' she said. 'I didn't mean to. I thought the gate was closed.'

He stood up and made a grab for the dog's collar, but it swerved its head and sprang back, ready to play. He made another move to catch hold of it, but the dog was off, chasing a smell in the grass.

'Get it! Catch him!' shouted David, and Angela, who was hugging her shoulders together, jerked forward in a halting, staccato manner, but the dog evaded her too and bounded onto the road where it looked back, tongue hanging out, waiting.

'Bloody dog! Bloody dog!' shouted David, his hand smarting in pain from where he had torn it on top of the wall.

'Come here, come here,' Angela called to it softly. 'Good boy, come on.'

But the dog turned on his heel and trotted off down the road, stopping to snuffle in a drain, before disappearing into some long grass.

'What the hell are we going to do now?' exclaimed David. Angela didn't answer, biting her lip and shying away from his anger.

'I'll get him.' Her lip trembled. 'I'll get him. It's my fault.'

'It's not your fault. I didn't mean...'

'No, Dad. It's true. I should have been more careful. I'm sorry, I'll get him.'

'I'm the one who's sorry. I don't know what happened.'

'Dad, stop it. Please, just stop it. You always do this.'

'Do what?'

'Apologise. I hate it. If you mean something, say it. Just *say* it. Don't say it and then say you didn't say it.'

'I'm sorry.'

She rolled her eyes, which were glistening with tears. '*Dad!* This is not one of your books. You can't go back and edit; you can't take back what has been said. You're not in control of the beginning and the end and the next chapter and who says what and why.'

'I...' he stopped and slumped against the wall. The hard granite dug into his back. He squeezed his hand. He wanted to feel pain, sharp pain, course through his body.

'Oh, Angela...' he began, but the pain was too much. It ran wildly through his body, swamping it with an unbearable agony, a torment of both physical suffering and overwhelming grief. At first, he tried to hold it back, to keep it in its place, but the torrent was too strong and fast and there was a relief, too, a peace, in letting go.

He cried in great racking sobs, letting his body double up under the weight of its sorrow. He let the tears come. Let his arms collapse limply next to him, let his head roll to the side. He felt arms around him and a face next to his.

'Angela,' he said. 'Angela...'

'I know, Dad,' she said, holding him close. 'I know.'

Early in the morning four days later, the lights of a taxi turned into the drive of the bed and breakfast and stopped outside the cottage.

'Taxi's here, Dad,' said Angela, putting down her mug of tea.

He looked across at her and nodded. It was unusual to see her dressed in something other than black. She had bought a brightly coloured T-shirt at Victoria Falls and red, green and gold wire earrings. He was surprised at how much more mature she suddenly looked and realised with a pang that she was nearly grown up.

'Mum messaged,' he said, looking down at his phone.

'Good,' she replied, not looking at him.

'She's looking forward to seeing us again.'

Angela nodded and stood up, scooping up the pile of passports and tickets.

They closed the door to the cottage and let the taxi driver place their two suitcases in the back of the taxi.

'Time to go, Dad,' said Angela, as the car moved down the road. She squeezed his arm.

David looked down at his phone and considered sending a reply to Nancy's message.

'Just leaving,' he tapped out. Then he stopped, his forefinger hovering over the keypad before adding: 'See you soon.'

When We Were Kings

Thabisani Ndlovu

But you, my friend, my brother, how can I forget you? Remember the challenge you made at the Palace Hotel Garden Bar, slapping the new Zimbabwean $50 note on the bar counter one pay day Friday and saying, 'If the two of us dakaza – recklessly spend and finish this money on food and drinks before midnight, I'll give you all of my salary for this month!' It was the highest denomination, released that month, crisp, with its clean new-money smell. You asked the barman to run a tab. 'We don't want to drink like poor wretched people, you know, the lot that Fanon speaks of,' you said and we laughed. Remember, the highest denomination before the $50 had been $20, the one with a picture of an elephant. That's why people used to say, smiling enough to outshine the sun, 'The elephant has fallen,' to refer to pay day. Well, there was no picture of an elephant on that $50 note but there it was, under the barman's counter, big as an elephant when the Hwange National Park has received good rains and all around is green trees and grass. If we failed to do justice to the elephant, we would invite other people we felt were fit enough to chop, hack and carve our elephant with us. Besides, we had other fifties packed so tightly in our wallets they could not breathe. We were rolling mfowethu.

But for now I continue to wade through tall grass, weaving my way amongst graves. I step more gingerly in places where they are not clearly marked. Like here. Just a few mounds and depressions. This one has a small black zinc plaque nailed to a rotting stick that might lie down any day. The white oil paint has flaked off so much I can't read what it was meant to say. I can only make out what I think would have been 'Moyo' and perhaps the year of death, '07' for 2007? This other one that has caved in so much it looks like a shallow bathtub only has the little aluminium tag that bears the grave number, stuck, I know, in the direction of the head. That's all. Dead and forgotten. No one returned to add more soil on top, following the inevitable warp after one rainy season in this cemetery. A metre deep, and you hit soft shale. Not even the beautiful graves are spared. Like this shiny marble one that is now lopsided – headstone, kerbs and the white pebbles inside the borders of the grave. For those that have sunk in more than others, big cracks show along the edges. I imagine if I stepped on one of these cracks, the whole thing will cave in and swallow me and I'll find it difficult to get out, with a broken leg or something and that would be the end of me. Too many movies maybe?

At around 8pm we ended up recruiting two women who did not need much persuasion to join in the drinking and dancing and dakazaring. We clapped our hands, threw them in the air, wound our waists to the thumping beat. Jumped like mad men wanting to pluck all the stars from the sky. We were no match for those two women. Those waists that moved as if the owners were boneless. The rest I can't quite remember. What is still clear, even today, is that we left the Palace in the early hours of the morning with the $50 still unfinished. Part of the elephant stubbornly remained. You told the barman, actually you shouted, that he could keep the change. 'Let's leave that for the poor,' you said, and laughed like only you could. Laughed with the assurance of a young man in his prime, not knowing of course, that a virus would be the end of you; that you would waste away and I would wonder if I was next.

We woke up in a strange place, somewhere out of town. The two women were cousins – very nice in that rural-respect, looking-for-a-husband sort of way. Or were they putting on a show? We might have been their long-gone husbands returned home. Why not? Why not indeed, like that hotel in Esigodini? Someone loved that phrase so much they named the hotel after it. We gave the two women their money, which was $15 each, five more than what they had asked for, and a further $10 to get us food. You insisted on eggs and fried chicken. You laughed and said, 'Isn't education great? Now we get to eat the chicken and the chicken-in-the-making, all at once.' It is true; we never grew up eating eggs for breakfast or at any other mealtime for

27

that matter. You had told me the only way you could eat any eggs was through stealing them from your mother's hens. The eggs were there so chicks could hatch out of them. I had told you I was a bit lucky, my Granny used to give me some eggs on the sly.

One day, you called from the bathroom and, when I opened the door slightly, you smiled, head partly buried in overflowing bath foam and said, 'Haven't I always told you, you useless sceptic, you Marechera spartan, that education is good? Now I can take a bath lying down in this sweet-smelling bubbly water. Nice scent, ha?' I shook my head and snorted, knowing that you had a point, which I would not have put so honestly. We had grown up taking a bath standing inside or beside a dish (the zinc ones made by the Vapostori) or a plastic bucket (the sort with a strong new-plastic smell, sold at Indian shops along Lobengula Street), depending on the size of the container. Yes, you made me realise the narrow escape we had made through our university education. We had escaped bathing next to a bucket. We had escaped the loud call of the municipal bottle store that our age mates heeded on a daily basis to guzzle drums and drums of masese, and the petty crimes that went with the habit of leaning against the walls of the bottle store as if fearing the walls might fall down if left unsupported. Nine in the morning to eight in the evening, our age mates boozing daily, asking for 'just one' from those with regular jobs or housebreaking to buy a few more. You and me, Khumbu, we were nothing more than disenchanted high school teachers just started work but all considered, we had escaped the bottle store. And more. We had escaped sleeping in our parents' kitchens or living rooms with four, five, six other siblings.

Even as I smile at these memories, I still can't find you. Grass grows tall and happy around and on most of the graves. Only a few have been tended, mostly the ones with elegant tombstones of marble and granite. We laid you close to a tree that drizzly morning. If I remember well, it must have been umsehla. But there is not a single tree now in sight, not one the size of the umsehla tree those many years ago, and certainly the giant tree it would have been now. So, many years later, it looks like all trees in this graveyard were chopped down for firewood and grass left to grow wild and happy.

Where are you, Khumbu my friend? I have come a long way and I can't just go back without seeing you. The cemetery has grown and I'm not so sure if I'm in the correct section. All around me is a sea of tall grass. And I keep looking, because you would have done the same for me, because only chance made me survive. I want to get angry at somebody, something. Then I think of how difficult it is these days for anyone to have even one dollar. Maybe the living are not neglecting the dead. I decide to think it is nobody's fault – maybe. I look up at the broody sky and decide these graves, most hidden in grass, some caving in, forgotten – all of this, is the rain's fault. Khumbu, the rain will find me here before I find your grave in this tall grass, if I ever find it. This lump, burning in my throat, needs cooling. I know it might be many more years before I swallow the pain of your grave lost in the tall grass. But hey, I'll pass through the Palace and have one for you where once we were kings on our teachers' salaries in Bulawayo, the City of Kings – of course, when the elephant fell.

In the Beauty of the Lilies

John Eppel

April Day, who had been born in April, was about to be buried in April. Eighty years, give or take her name, separated the month of birth from the month of death. The place, however, was not different. She lay in state in her bedroom, once her parents' bedroom, on the same bed she had been born. One person, a midwife, had witnessed her birth; no one had witnessed her death – unless you could call her tabby, Tabby, a person.

The cassia trees that lined Cecil Avenue were in full, fruity yellow flower, their dense canopies providing a welcome shade for the endless procession of men, women and children who relied on their legs to take them from one locked gate to another; or from one gathering of white-robed Vapostori to another; or from one cardboard box vendor to another.

Earlier that morning, shortly before April had closed her eyes forever, a choir of Heuglin's robins had held her fading attention; and in the darkling landscape of her mind she might have recalled their gorgeous orange plumage and distinctive white eye stripes. But that wasn't the only music she might have been listening to; for in the portable CD player next to her bedside table, the last track, 21, the most glorious tenor voice in recording history was bringing the 'Ingemisco' from Verdi's *Requiem* to an end. No, not Enrico Caruso (earth), not Beniamino Gigli (water), not Jussi Björling (air), not Franco Corelli (fire), but a combination of the four elements, a quintessence: Thulani Khumalo. He would cancel his final La Scala performance as Pinkerton in Puccini's *Madama Butterfly* in order to sing at Miss Day's funeral in Bulawayo.

Her room was sparsely furnished. Against the wall opposite her bed was a wardrobe in dark wood, with a tarnished full length mirror, which, right now, reflected Miss Day's shamelessly exposed nostrils and the wiry mole hair at the base of her chin. The whole exuded a whiff of cologne and mildewed shoes. On the window ledge stood a brass vase with no fewer than twelve different specimens of wild flowers poking out of its dented lip. These flowers had been gathered a few days before from the encroaching bush of Miss Day's yard situated in the suburb of Hillside. Next to the vase was a red Smythson (of Bond Street) note book, A5, which contained sketches and notes on many wild grasses and flowers. These grew in the vicinity of Bulawayo. The last entered sketch was labelled, *eragrostis cilianensis*, followed by the common name: 'stink lovegrass'. April Day had been an amateur botanist. Professionally, she had been a music teacher, the proud possessor (thanks to Grandfather O'Casey) of a Bechstein baby grand.

In a framed black and white photograph hanging from the picture rail on the wall opposite the window, her only child smiled stiffly. That picture had been taken shortly before Piccolo had been kidnapped by his English father, Sergeant-Major Blushington. The child must have been about five years old. He was wearing a sailor suit. In his left hand was a miniature Union Jack, in his right a golliwog with staring eyes and fuzzy hair. The only other decoration on that wall was a large print, signed, of the great African American singer – that sweet rumble of thunder – Paul Robeson.

On the wall above her headboard was a framed print of a mural depicting John Brown as a flame-haired giant, arms stretched in the form of a cross, with a bible in his left hand and a rifle in his right. The middle ground depicts the clash of pro-slavery and anti-slavery forces. In the background there is a tornado squaring up to a raging inferno. Miss Day chose the picture, not for its allegorical intent but because, she told Tabby, John Brown resembled her Irish grandfather, O'Casey. There was another, more sentimental, reason. The print is entitled: TRAGIC PRELUDE.

When April started teaching at White Rhino High, she was already way past retirement age; but music teachers were as scarce as hens' teeth in Bulawayo, so she was employed on a contract basis, one year at a time.

She was grateful for the job because she had lost her life savings some years back when her bank bolted its doors.

One Sunday she and her friend and colleague, Clementine Ndimande, decided to go on a picnic in the Matobo communal lands some thirty kilometres south of Bulawayo. It was the last Sunday of the school holidays, promising to be fine and mild. Being January, in the middle of a fairly good rainy season, there should be wild flowers in bloom. Clementine, a maths teacher, was many years younger than April, in her fifties. She was a widow, and her three children, all with families of their own, were living in the Diaspora.

They packed a basket with cheese and tomato sandwiches, ginger snaps, and a thermos flask of sweet milky tea. They took the old Gwanda road in Clementine's yellow Datsun Sunny, and stopped along the way to visit Mzilikazi's memorial. He was known as the Lion of the North and he was the founder of the amaNdebele nation. He was a Khumalo.

The muted sound of a cow bell reached them and they continued on their way towards the eastern Matobo hills. They found a spot beside a stream, running quite strongly at this time of year. They selected a delicious patch of shade under a mobola plum tree, took out two folding chairs from the boot of the car, spread a checked tablecloth on the ground, and proceeded to unpack their picnic. Almost immediately a yellow-billed kite appeared out of nowhere, settled itself on the topmost branch of a dead pod mahogany, and waited patiently for scraps. Clearly other picnickers had preceded April and Clementine to this lovely spot. Both women sighed with pleasure as they sank into their chairs and looked about them. The only cloud in the sky was a fading vapour trail connecting Bulawayo to Johannesburg. In the distance a Cape turtle dove kept repeating its three haunting notes. The friends munched happily on their sandwiches.

Presently a boy appeared, seemingly from nowhere. He was about twelve years old and he was wearing the uniform of a North American mission school run by the Church of Christ. He was incompletely dressed, however, for he wore no shoes and stockings, no cap, and no tie. He was covered in dust. The teachers from White Rhino High assumed he was going to beg from them, but they were wrong. He asked for a crust of bread to feed to the yellow-billed kite, which had taken to the air. 'Watch this,' he said in English. He launched the crust;

the kite swooped and caught it just when gravity had begun to reverse its trajectory. April offered the boy a ginger snap but he politely declined. Then he said, 'Would you like to hear me sing?' The teachers said they would. He gave them a bright smile, and in the purest treble April had ever heard, he sang:

John Brown's body lies a-mouldering in the grave;
John Brown's body lies a-mouldering in the grave;
John Brown's body lies a-mouldering in the grave:
His soul's marching on!
Glory, glory, hallelujah! Glory, glory, hallelujah!
Glory, glory, hallelujah! His soul's marching on!

April prompted him on the second stanza: 'He's gone to be a soldier in the army of the Lord...' and they sang it together through to the end.

April was enthralled. She asked the boy his name – Thulani. Would he like to sing before the school children at White Rhino High? Vigorous nodding. Once term started she would make arrangements. She would get in touch with senior staff at the mission school where Thulani was a boarder. He could spend a night or two with her or Mrs Ndimande, and she was sure her school would provide transport. The boy then said he wanted to show them something, and motioned them to follow him.

They walked along the stream a little way before following a cattle path towards a low-lying granite hill covered in yellow and orange lichen. In cracks where soil had gathered, ferns and mosses grew interspersed with aloes and resurrection plant. Brightly coloured rock lizards, camouflaged by the lichen, were sunning themselves everywhere. They were aware of being stared at by half-hidden dassies, elephant shrews, and leguaans.

April smelt them before she saw them. Just over the top of the hill, in a damp, sandy area to the right was what Thulani wanted to show them: a crowd, a host of vlei lilies, hundreds of them in full flower, white with pink keels. The combined sight and scent was breathtaking, overwhelming for April who burst into tears and spontaneously took the boy into her arms. 'My family is buried there,' said the boy.

'Your family?' She let go of him and stared into his eyes.

'My mother, my father, my uncle, and my two sisters.'

'What happened?'

'Soldiers.'

'Soldiers?'

'Soldiers with red hats. I was away at the mission. Our neighbour told me. The soldiers said my uncle was a dissident, and because he was living with us we were also dissidents. They locked all of them in a hut and set fire to it.'

April and Clementine looked at each other helplessly. Then they looked back at the field of lilies, beginning to sway in a sudden gust of warm air. They offered their condolences and promised the boy they would not forget him. It was with heavy hearts that they returned to Bulawayo, and prepared to face the new school year.

Not only did April manage to persuade her school to invite Thulani to perform at Monday assembly, but she persuaded the Board of Trustees to award him a music scholarship, which included tuition in all subjects. He was to board with Mrs Ndimande while April would see to his voice training. The Church of Christ saw the move as beneficial to the child, especially since he was an orphan, so they gave the move their blessing.

At his first assembly performance, Thulani did not sing 'John Brown's Body', he sang 'Hear My Prayer', and he learnt it by listening over and over again to Miss Day's 1927 recording by the famous boy soprano, Ernest Lough. That morning, in the school hall, with more than 700 girls and boys in attendance, you could have heard a pin drop. The entire school was stunned by the ineffable beauty of Thulani's voice. He was soon in great demand, not just at school functions, but at weddings, funerals, and baptisms. He flourished in the foster care of his two mothers, and a community that appreciated his gift.

The treble is a short-lived range. A year after attending White Rhino High, Thulani's voice began to break, and his music teacher became very apprehensive about the future. Nevertheless she continued to coach him, insisting in particular on breath control. Teacher and student adapted to a lower, more limited range. In Miss Day's experience, pre-pubertal boys with treble voices tended to become baritones or basses, while those with alto voices tended to become tenors. When the adolescent voice began to seal its cracks, about a year after the first signs of breaking, it became clear to April that Thulani, against expectation, was becoming a tenor. He had a natural ability to blend head and chest notes, and it wasn't long before he could produce a high C and then a high D, with a timbre that reminded April of a warm blade passing through butter. She also taught him to play the piano to the level of Grade 8, with the Royal Schools of Music in London.

Thulani stayed on at White Rhino High until he had completed his A Levels. Then, with Miss Day's support, he found a place at a university in South Africa where he majored in voice and piano. Gradually they began to lose touch with each other; but the less April heard from her protégé in person, the more she began to hear about him in public. He got his first solo role with the Cape Town Opera company, as Rodolfo in Puccini's *La Bohème*. It wasn't long before he was touring the great opera houses of the world, increasing his repertoire, accommodating his flexible voice to lyric, *spinto*, and dramatic roles. Like Caruso, he could sing light bass roles; like Gedda he could hit the high F note in Bellini's 'Credeasi Misera' without whistling. After ten years on the circuit he was being universally acclaimed as the greatest tenor in recording history.

When Thulani heard from an old school friend that Miss Day had died, he dropped all his appointments and caught the earliest flight home to Bulawayo. The funeral service was to take place at the crematorium the following day. Clementine Ndimande had made all the arrangements. She was thrilled when her foster child phoned her from the Oliver Tambo airport in Johannesburg to say that he would attend the funeral service and would like to sing for his departed music teacher. He also begged her to take him to his family home in the Matobo hills. There was something he needed to do.

Clementine was at the Bulawayo airport to meet Thulani. She had driven there in her yellow Datsun Sunny so that they could go straight out to the communal lands. They hugged each other speechlessly, and there were tears, not only from the old school teacher's eyes. Clementine had packed a picnic lunch of cheese and tomato sandwiches, ginger snaps, and sweet milky tea. They said very little to each other on the drive out. The corrugations on the old Gwanda road were worse than ever but nothing much else had changed. When they passed the Mzilikazi memorial Thulani breathed, 'My ancestor.' Mrs Ndimande squeezed his hand.

They arrived at the old picnic spot and Thulani, after a quick snack, said he wanted to see if there were any lilies in bloom. It was unlikely this late in the season. He left Clementine under the mobola plum while he made his way to the granite hill. Before reaching the summit, he picked up the characteristic scent, and his heart began to pound. There was one umbel left in flower, one which grew on the mass grave of his family. Thulani gave thanks to his ancestors, plucked the umbel, which sprouted four flowers, and returned with it to the picnic spot. 'It's for Miss Day,' he said.

There were about forty people at the funeral service, all teachers and pupils from White Rhino High. It was a secular service. Clementine read a poem, and three of the pupils read tributes. Thulani placed the slightly wilted vlei lily on Miss Day's coffin, and then cleared his thoat to sing. The congregation were expecting 'Ave Maria' or 'Panis Angelicus' or 'Agnus Dei', but they got the tune of 'John Brown's Body' sung to the words of 'Battle Hymn of the Republic'. They all agreed that it was a stirring send off for the ancient music teacher, and that Thulani Khumalo had a lovely voice for that kind of singing.

North-South Jet Lag

Melissa Tandiwe Myambo

I was on the phone with a so-called journalist, a Mr Thomas from *The Economist*, when I heard a knocking on the French doors. As usual, he wanted a pithy sound bite to sum up the complexities of the tumultuous Indonesian telecom industry but, when I explained to him that I could not merely give an oversimplified thumbs-up or thumbs-down, he started to hee and haw. What an incorrigible twit! I hung up on him mid-faff and made my way to the south side of the villa.

Through the glass doors, I could see Liezel looking very agitated in the bright morning light, the tangible sun rays already at an almost vertical angle, the wind on this side of the mountain whipping horizontally across the sparkling water of the swimming pool. I opened the door. Liezel's eyes were scrunched up, disapprobation flushing her cheeks. Her measured, flattened vowels had a hard edge, 'Good morning, Mr Quintin, may I just have a word with you? I realize you've only just arrived back but... Have you seen the note I'd left for you? The Dew Drop Estate Body Corporate honestly thinks–'

Liezel was my neighbour of the last four months, although I had barely seen her between my perpetual travels. In fact, I had only spoken to her properly on one occasion when she had popped by to request a donation of five hundred for the Dew Drop Estate's annual fundraiser for orphans living with HIV/AIDS. I had given her fifteen thousand. Her intensely blue eyes had widened into a grateful, almost worshipful, smile but I shook my head. It was both a worthy cause and a wise investment in my neighbours' gratitude, which hopefully would translate into a live-and-let-live sentiment, a quid pro quo that would forgive my sometimes extravagant lifestyle.

37

'Won't you come in, Liezel. And have some tea.' I have a quasi-religious devotion to the civilizing ritual of tea drinking.

'Ya no, I wouldn't want to be a bother. I just stopped by to say that it's best not to rock the boat. You understand, it sets a bad precedent. The next thing, they will all be expecting the same.'

I had not seen her note hence I'd no idea what she was talking about, so I opened the door further and held out my hand in invitation. I am a rich man and a big one to boot. Very few people disregard my wishes.

Liezel scooped up her compact brown and white dog and followed me across the marble floor my wife had had imported from Tuscany at great expense, her flip flops making hollow echoing sounds, the mirrored walls presenting her with myriad reflections of her new-mother haggardness. She clutched the writhing terrier with one hand and tried to pat down her wind-blown hair sticking up at odd angles.

We descended two shallow steps into the area my wife insisted on calling 'the sunken lounge', which offered a view of the swimming pool with its miniature waterfall emerging from the rock garden. I opened the French doors as I pointed Liezel towards the red leather chaise, inappropriate furniture for this sun-filled room. 'Patience,' I called into the intercom. 'Patience, please bring Madam some tea – shall we have the Mackwoods – and those nice almond biscuits. That's champion. And also those coconut macaroons if they've not gone stale.'

The violet circles under Liezel's tired eyes were so dark they looked like bruises. 'Isn't her name Precious?'

Suddenly, I could not remember. My packed bags were still in the hall as I had only just returned from the World Economic Forum's Annual Meeting in Switzerland and I had not slept for over 48 hours. 'Well, the important thing is that she knows I am talking to her.' I sat down in the red leather armchair opposite her and put my feet on the crystal coffee table – my third wife's taste is incredibly kitsch but what can a husband do except to endure and pay the credit card bill. It had been a long flight and my ankles were swollen. 'Now, why don't you start at the beginning again and tell me exactly what the problem is.'

Liezel sighed tiredly. I looked at her sympathetically. She reminded me of my eldest son's wife. They were probably both around thirty. 'First of all, how is your baby?'

Liezel's small mouth puckered, then pulled into a line as she propped the little dog on her lap, 'He's not sleeping much, hey. Everyone says he should be sleeping through the night by now but...'

I looked at her bosom. She must have had quite nice breasts before breast-feeding but now they were drooping like deflated balloons underneath her thin white sundress. 'May I tell you something, Liezel. It's only the first child who really matters. After this, it's just more of the same. Believe me, I have six children. But you see, it's with the first that you experience it all for the first time. You may not realize it now but this is a time in which you're intensely alive. Yes, you're exhausted but this is when you're making your bid for a quasi-immortality as you see your own genetic material growing into a little person. Do you see what I mean.'

'What an appalling statement, Mr Quintin!' She stopped suddenly, patted the dozing dog's heaving rib cage, 'I don't mean to sound cheeky but I am sure one loves all one's children.'

'Oh no, I misspoke. Please do call me Alastair by the way – I am 56, well almost 57, but I like to flatter myself that I look younger than my years. Perhaps I am not quite as good-looking as Sean Connery but I have all my own teeth still and even most of my hair. I have an iPod and I listen to Reggaeton and K-Pop, so please do call me by my first name. You love all your children but it's only the first one that can give you that kick! How often do you feel truly alive, Liezel?'

It was a genuine question but her response was disappointing.

'Well, these days I go around feeling half dead mostly from lack of sleep.' She touched her almost flat belly, smiling lopsidedly. 'And anyways, I'm expecting again. Number Two should be coming along by the end of winter so the hormones also make me nap rather a lot.'

'Then I have a proposition for you. One year from today, let's resume this discussion. Whether Number Two is a boy or a girl makes no difference. You will see that the instinct to reproduce is fulfilled by the first. Subsequent offspring are mere photocopies of the original child.'

She wriggled on the chaise, 'I doubt that very much. Perhaps also your being a man makes you think that but I'm quite sure one loves all one's children the same.' Her blue eyes darkened to a thundercloud, 'I am thirty-three years old and I think I know what's what, Mr Quintin!'

Her little dog woke up in response to her tart tone and started its high-pitched yapping. Jack Russells are such nervous creatures.

'Alastair, please! I hope I haven't offended you. Well, at least, not irrevocably. You probably don't know much about me besides what those scurrilous curs who count themselves as reporters write about me but there is a wide ravine between my public persona and my private self. Do you know, for example, that I've been at an utter standstill for perhaps 23 years?'

She had no inkling, of course, no idea that for so long I had been travelling without moving. An unshakeable stasis had descended without warning the day my net worth had doubled that of my last worthy rival.

After I had made my first hundred million, I quickly set about acquiring all the material accessories, all the clichés – fast cars, century-old cognac, Beluga caviar, a sleek yacht, a house in the South of France; I replaced my first wife from Birmingham with a new trophy wife from Barcelona (nine years my junior and my rival's spouse to boot!) and I eventually replaced her with my third and current Chongqing wife who is 17 years younger. Once Operation Acquire Loads of Worldly Goods was completed, I battled the onset of my middle-age crisis by testing the limits of mental resilience and bodily exertion with speed and endurance tests – triathlons, hang gliding, kite surfing, abseiling. After I made my first billion, I set up the first of three philanthropic organizations funding feature and documentary films in the hopes of promoting political and social change in the world, which would in turn produce a mirror effect on the inside. But you see, it's so very boring once you've done it all.

My eldest son's wife is a psychologist, or at least she was trained as one, and she said to me once that wealthy men start out seeking tangible stuff and, once they've accumulated all they can, they start searching out those intangibles – extreme sensation, status, social impact. But how long can cocktails with prime ministers and media appearances with teenaged celebrities continue to intrigue?

The little dog jumped off the chaise, its claws clattering onto the marble floor, and it started sniffing at the potted bamboo plant. 'Graça, Graça, come here, sit!'

'Don't fuss about the dog, let her do as she likes. I am a man with everything who implicitly then has nothing, for it is only in having

40

some things and lacking others that one has *anything*. Do you see what I mean?'

'Ya no, I think that perhaps, Mr Quin... Alastair, I think we must address... well to come to the root of the problem. The Estate Body Corporate feels that we could have a mini-revolution on our hands unless... I won't mince my words, hey, since you are obviously a very direct man... unless you reduce your workers' salaries to be in line with what we all are paying our domestics.'

'Bravo! That was absolutely champion. Here I am talking at the most abstract level – essential intangibles – and you've come back at me with the most concrete, most prosaic of concerns. Money! Of course, in a philosophical sense, money too is an abstraction, a value assigned to a tang–'

'Well, I am an accountant, for God's sake! What do you expect me to do with all this airy-fairy nonsense? I'm quite busy as well and don't have time for this.' She tugged at the dog's collar until it yelped. Shaking her head as if to dispel her crossness, she inhaled deeply, 'I am sorry, I just haven't slept much for... well, ages now, and I'm very hormonal as well. Anyways, I was an accountant before I had the baby and, since I'm a stay-at-home mum now, I have joined the Estate Body Corporate and this issue has come up and quite frankly, excuse my directness, but it's causing quite a lot of dissension, hey. Your domestics are getting significantly more than any of ours, or the guards at the front gate who are working twelve-hour shifts. And you know, Precious is cousins with my house girl, Fadzi. So you can imagine the tension, they're doing the same job but–' She abruptly stopped speaking and discomfort danced in her flushed cheeks as she looked at a point behind me.

I turned my head, 'Ahh, right on cue. We have been patiently awaiting your precious arrival on the scene.'

'Good morning, Mr Alastair. Good morning, Madam.'

She looked exactly the part, middle-aged, dressed in a pink and grey uniform with an apron tied around her waist and her hair covered with a matching pink scarf. I had never really looked at her before but now I saw that she had quite an attractive heart-shaped face and very lively eyes. An excellent idea occurred to me.

I quickly removed my feet from the table so Patience/Precious could put the tray down. The poor woman had no idea she was the object of Liezel's self-righteous rancour and, as she bent over, looking at Graça with some antipathy, the terrier started yapping excitedly again and charged towards her.

'Shush, Graça, shush. Come here, sit, come,' said Liezel, patting her lap invitingly, as Precious recoiled from the dog's cold wet nose.

'Thank you for the tea. Now, are you patiently precious or preciously patient?'

'Come again.'

I beamed at her, baring my expensively whitened teeth all the way back to the molars, 'Please do join us for a cuppa. Sit down, do. Sit right there.' I indicated the armchair to the left of Liezel.

She hesitated, 'I have had my tea with Phineas, the garden boy.'

'Well, have some biscuits then.'

'But I ate bread and I even put some of that margarine.'

'Oh do sit down, will you. I want to discuss something with you.'

Liezel waggled her eyebrows at me inquiringly but I focused my attention on Precious as she perched on the edge of the armchair, keeping her incongruously large hands in her lap. She was a lean and wiry woman, pulsating with energy – the things she lacked imbuing her with that enviable sense of urgency. I could see her left heel tapping out a staccato rhythm on the veined marble.

I leant forward and looked her straight in the eye and then did the same to Liezel. This is the way I typically begin board meetings in order to elicit both respect and pliancy. 'Now, please state your name so that the minutes may duly reflect it.'

She looked nonplussed but then smiled prettily, revealing small, widely-spaced teeth. 'Precious.' Then she added dryly, 'It's the fourth time you ask me that, Mr Alastair.'

I laughed boyishly although I was slightly abashed. 'I beg your pardon, Precious. I dare say I have been quite busy, travelling up and down, but I shan't forget again. Precious, this is Madam Liezel.'

'How are you today, Madam?'

Liezel nodded, but I could see she was a bit discomfited, 'I'm fine, Precious. How are you?' Her voice rose into a squeak on the 'you,' the 'are' almost swallowed. 'We already know each other, Alastair, because Fadzi is your cousin, isn't it, Precious?'

'She's the wife of my brother.'

I looked from one to the other, 'Ah yes, that should ease us into this discussion. Prior acquaintances etc., practically blood relatives.' I laughed heartily. 'Precious, Madam Liezel has come to me this morning with a slight problem. It appears your salary is too high, higher than that of the other esteemed domestics working in the other sixteen villas in Dew Drop Estate. Madam Liezel has proposed that I lower your salary to be on a par with the others. Is that an adequate summary of your viewpoint, Liezel?'

Liezel blushed a furious blotchy red and squeezed Graça to her chest until she yelped. She opened and closed her mouth like the proverbial fish and that's when I felt *it*! After so long, a topographical shifting in my internal geography, a stagnant pond suddenly transformed into a thundering waterfall! Or was it just that I had hardly slept on the plane?

'But my son,' stuttered Precious whose open face now wore a startled, wary expression. Her voice trailed off.

'Ladies, my dear ladies, I think we should approach this as rational human beings and discuss this in an open and respectful manner so we can debate all sides of the issue. Isn't that the way it should be done.'

Precious looked as if I had shoved her in front of a firing squad and seemed to be choking. Liezel was wearing her little dog like a fur collar as if she wanted to hide her face, which was fast becoming a uniform eggplant colour.

'Let me pour you both some tea. Try some macaroons.' I poured milk into the two teacups and then added the steaming tea. I handed her one cup and Liezel was obliged to release the captive dog to accept the other, although she glared at me bitterly.

Precious tried to stand up claiming that I didn't have a cup but I told her to remain seated. My tea could wait. There was a deliciously fractious episode under way. I laughed heartily. 'Well, the question remains, how much is too much? Yesterday, in Davos, I gave the keynote lecture for the afternoon panel co-sponsored by the Who is John Galt Society, 'Creativity, Capacity Building and Heartfelt Capitalism.' I began with an anecdote that I will share with you both. It was meant, I assure you, to provide the audience with ample food for thought. The Managing Director of the IMF and the President of the European Central Bank came up to warmly congratulate me afterwards. Of course, what I said may have flown over the heads of the obligatory

Hollywood celebs who always pepper such events, I have no idea. That Angela Jolie was there. Now, she rather intrigues me: she plays the sexy assassin in all her films and makes a mint but then advocates for love and peace. Rather hypocritical if you ask me. But now I'm curio–'

Liezel squinted her eyes at me rather warily but I could see she was intrigued, rather against her will. 'Was Angelina there with Brad? Or are they divorced now?'

Precious was leaning so far forward she almost slid off the armchair. Truly, a captive audience.

I laughed, 'Yes, I believe so but I'm not sure whether he also attended my lecture.'

'And the children?' asked Precious.

'Not a clue.'

'They have five little ones, hey,' murmured Liezel. 'I wonder how many nannies they have.'

'They have six children,' said Precious with some authority, smiling her toothy smile. 'Even one of them is an African. I myself think it's good because they have plenty money to look after however many children, so they can adopt as many as they like.'

Hee-haw, hee-haw, faff, faff, faff. But I let this conversation continue for a little while as I could see it was helping them to relax a bit, but finally I intervened, 'To proceed: I opened my lecture with this rather instructive anecdote. At the height of the financial crisis, I was in New York for a board meeting. Walking down Fifth Avenue, a tramp stuck a paper cup in front of me. One should always give the less fortunate a helping hand but, on that day, as it happens, I had yet to withdraw US currency and hence all I had in my wallet was pounds sterling. I said, very politely mind you, because I imagine the gentleman was my senior by some years, 'I beg your pardon, sir. I don't have any change.' And do you know what he said to me?' Here, I changed the shape of my lips to approximate his accent which sounded as if his mouth were full of marshmallows, ''What's wrong with cash? What, like I don't take dollars!''

And even then, in the retelling of my retelling, I had to hold my sides as I laughed with the mirthfulness of it, but Liezel's lips retracted into a flat line and Precious merely raised her eyebrows, which were pencilled in with a brown liner only marginally darker than her skin.

'So I said – completely truthfully, mind you – that I didn't have dollars but only British pounds. The gentleman looked at me derisively and said, 'More like a pound of flesh.' And I retorted, 'All the world's a stage... And one man in his time plays many parts.' And then he went off, grumbling to himself. Imagine that!'

The audience had chortled merrily except for the President of the Who is John Galt Society, who had frowned at my mention of giving to the needy. But what he does not understand is that in order to maintain societal balance, we cannot afford to have a segment of the population too far below the median income. By the same token, there should be no restrictions on allowing the talented to rise as high as possible, because that will automatically pull up the median. I looked from Liczel's dour expression to Precious, who seemed to be drowning in the milky depths of her tea, her heel in her thin-soled canvas shoe still tapping out its jaunty rhythm.

'You see, this gentleman down on his fortune had raised an important point. When giving, what amount is too much? We live in a world in which we have to balance the needs of the poor with the incentive to work hard. It's a fine balance, not easily achieved. I have made my fortune by investing in the inefficient stock markets of emerging economies, from Indonesia to Brazil to here in South Africa. High risk, high returns, as they say, but the potential for great losses always persists. Throughout my career, I have sought out new frontiers for capital investment while diversifying my investment portfolio such that safety and risk do not cancel out growth.'

I realized I was losing my audience. But just then, the next-door neighbour's tortoiseshell cat stalked in through the French doors, tiptoeing very daintily on her white paws. For some reason, the cat terrified Graça, who scrambled under the chaise. Precious jumped up and tried to shoo the cat back outside.

'Leave it, Precious. The house is becoming a veritable menagerie.' I was amused by the dog's reaction.

But Precious shook her head, 'Its hair will go everywhere.' She clucked her tongue as she clapped her hands to scare the cat back outside. Liezel tried to entice Graça out from under the chaise but the silly little dog was growling fearfully.

'Patience, sit down and drink your tea will you. You haven't even had one sip. Liezel, leave that nervous nelly. She will come out eventually. To proceed: I have been extraordinarily successful in outperforming the market because I have always hired the best and the brightest and, as I explain in my latest book, *Let Cream Rise*, I incentivize them by offering, what seems to the uninitiated, excessively lavish bonuses. One's goal is to enhance the conditions in which creative output is maximized. Those who dare to reverse the downward force of gravity must be duly recognized and handsomely rewarded. One must allow talent to rise to the top but keep them hungry too, wanting more success, greater conquests.'

Neither woman was paying me any attention, thus missing out on the distilled wisdom of almost forty years of business experience. When Graça finally crept out from under the chaise, Liezel scooped her up and cradled the trembling dog against her chest as if she were a babe in arms. Precious again held the teacup in her hands but still was not drinking anything. Outside, Phineas the gardener appeared in faded blue overalls, a rusty watering can in his left hand. As he bent to weed the flowerbed adjacent to the swimming pool, he suddenly caught sight of our odd little assembly.

'Good morning, Baas, welcome back! Good morning, Madam.' He said something to Precious in their own language but she didn't respond. He seemed a tad thick but otherwise quite a jolly fellow, but then again, gardening is both relaxing and refreshing for milder personality types.

I allowed the silence to grow, giving them time to refocus on the matter at hand. Phineas fiddled about amongst the recently planted orange and purple Bird of Paradise flowers, the only wise decision my wife had made regarding this property.

Originally, she had asked for a 'simple country bungalow' because we already had half-a-dozen penthouses but, somewhere along the way, she had persuaded me to buy this suburban villa as our winter home although, when it is winter in England, here of course it is summer. Meanwhile, as soon as I forked over the cash to buy the place, peanuts compared to real estate prices elsewhere, she spent a fortune renovating and redecorating and then buggered off to Singapore. Supposedly to visit her sister who has a new baby, but I know better. No matter. By the time I married her, beautiful women no longer produced any internal momentum so what do I care if she takes a lover or two. I would rather be here. Besides Singapore is so far West. Cape Town is more or less a straight shot down the Greenwich Meridian. I wonder if technically there is such a thing as North-South jet lag?

Precious chewed the inside of her cheek and finally began somewhat tentatively, 'But Mr Alastair, what substance is talent that makes it rise to the top? Is it cork–'

And I thought she hadn't been listening. The both of them are rather literal-minded, I must say. 'Talent... talent is that indefinable, always scarce, je ne sais quoi, which somehow, some way, always rises to the top. Like steam. Once you hit boiling point, evaporation occurs, steam rises. My job is to make sure it is always boiling.'

Precious nodded and shook her head at the same time, her dark brown eyes aglow, 'But with water droplets, for example, surface evaporation can occur below boiling point. The amount of energy it takes to transform a substance from a liquid to a gaseous state depends very much on the substance itself.'

I clapped my hands enthusiastically, 'Precisely! It is up to me to create the correct conditions for a certain amount of evaporation to occur, provided of course that I have the right substance.'

Liezel glowered at me, her pale eyes scrunched up again. The high colour was slowly ebbing from her face, 'I'm afraid I am quite lost.'

'Have some more tea! Precious, please pour Madam Liezel some more tea. Help yourself to a biscuit. My dear Liezel, we are ruminating upon the necessary conditions for success, which depends upon talent rising to the top.'

'What's that got to do with boiling points and evaporation?'

'Why, everything, of course!'

Precious twitched on the edge of the armchair, 'But Mr Alastair, evaporation is not the end of the cycle. Condensation occurs, the gaseous state returns to liquid. Water falls back to the earth.'

'But producing constant evaporation without reaching the point of saturation, that's what I do best.'

Liezel's temper flared again like a mini conflagration, 'Honestly, I haven't got the foggiest notion of what you're going on about! I wish I had time to sit around and discuss this more but I haven't slept properly for, well, let's see, over a year and a half, and this circular discussion over tea and almond biscuits is an absolute waste of time. I have to go and feed the baby before Fadzi puts him down for his nap. Precious, I'm sorry, hey, but the point is – and I hate to have to say it like this –

but the point is that you're getting four hundred more a month than Fadzi and the other domestics and maybe for someone with British pounds,' she gesticulated in my general direction, 'that's not a lot but for us, with South African rands, that's quite substantial. And Fadzi is not only cleaning and doing all the washing but is my part-time nanny as well. Of course I believe in fair wages but the point is that, here in the Estate, all the other domestics are making the same salary, and I think it's a fair salary, hey, so it's causing quite a lot of tension with you and Phineas getting so much more than the others.' Her tone was sharp, 'I mean, obviously it's up to you in the final analysis, Alastair, but...'

This impassioned speech seemed to leave her breathless and, as if to emulate her, Graça's pink tongue emerged as she started to pant.

Precious looked down at her clasped hands but her left heel was still drumming on the cool marble.

'What do you say, Precious?'

Precious' eyelids suddenly flew open and the whites of her eyes reminded me of a baulking horse, frothing at the bit, longing to throw her rider, but her voice was steady. 'I used to be a biology teacher before I came here to South Africa to look for work after the economy became too bad. I have my working papers, I am not an illegal. I have a son at the University of Zimbabwe and I must send him funds because now everything is too expensive. Here, they don't want my qualifications even though there is a shortage of teachers, so I must look for the work that pays the best.'

Hence boiling points and condensation. I was reminded of London cabbies. Eastern Europeans with degrees in chemical engineering from their formerly socialist countries but, due to utter backwardness, they would end up behind the wheel. Precious' resigned voice contained all the fatigue of that long journey south to the tip of the continent. Suddenly, she pushed her narrow hips back into the armchair as if leaning back from the ledge.

'My uncle is working as a waiter in a café in Rondebosch and his wife is working in a nail salon in Sea Point but I am working here because Mr Alastair pays me a living wage and this is a maximum security complex so I am not worried about tsotsis.'

Liezel interrupted, her tone now wheedling, 'That's spot on, Precious. Our locals have such a culture of entitlement but Zimbabwee-ans like you are just so grateful, hey. That's exactly it. Here in the complex you are safe from tsotsis! But imagine if the locals, and you know how our locals resent you foreigners, hey, imagine now if they heard you were making four hundred above a *generous* house girl's salary? What would they say? And the problem for you Zimbabwee-ans is that the Malawians will do it so much more cheaply. And they're very hard-working, hey. If you have a Malawian garden boy he doesn't mind also doing some ironing or washing the dishes when the house girl is off.' She looked back to me again, 'So frankly, demand is high for foreign help but the supply is more than adequate.'

I almost chuckled at Liezel's application of basic market principles to the petri dish economy of the Dew Drop Estate. But I didn't want to interrupt. I was thoroughly fascinated!

Precious nodded slowly but her heel abandoned its even drumbeat and began to vibrate frenetically, 'Ya but it's true. South Africans have a culture of entitlement but we Zimbabweans are hard workers. Me, I work sometimes eight or eleven or fifteen hours when Madam comes from Singapore with guests. But I have incentive to work hard because I know my salary can buy me mealie meal and sometimes meat at month-end. So I don't mind because there are many ways of doing the same job – you can take very long over a small thing, like twenty minutes to change the sheets or you can do it in five minutes. In twenty minutes, I can make the bed, scrub the bathtub and still have time to wash the windows. Other house girls spend the whole day just on polishing the floor.'

It was almost as if she was talking to herself now.

'Some people work many hours but they don't get paid a lot, others work less but get paid too much. If you're a football player, you get paid a lot, but if you clean toilets at the station, at month-end, you can't even buy cooking oil after paying for transport. I have my education but no-one wants it here so I have to work to eat.'

'And send your son money,' I added.

She shrugged her shoulders, her heel stilled. 'When he was small if he caught a cold I would put my mouth to his nostrils and suck all the mucus out. I–'

Liezel's tone was gentler now, maternal, 'Precious, I hope you know I am not being racialistic, hey. You know that. But what I am saying to you is that you must just understand that here in Dew Drop

Estate, we want to have a calm and safe life. All the members of the Body Corporate are concerned about this, including Mr Sithole from number seven. You know him, hey. It's not *just* the white homeowners who feel like this. All of us don't want trouble and with this wage differential, well, you can see, it's quite difficult, hey, I mean... the tension. I just don't think we want to rock the boat.'

I thought about Liezel's boat, about the forces that would cause it to rock and how she wanted just what most people do, smooth sailing, and all the other related metaphors we use to maintain the status quo. Outside, the wind noisily shifted direction, battering against the firm green stalks of the Bird of Paradise flowers. Suddenly, I realized it was almost eleven. Well, they had both had their say and a very entertaining morning it had been, but my pilot was on standby. I was due in Victoria Falls, a four-hour flight northwards, to meet my third-born son who had inherited his Spanish mother's good looks and my love of the thrill. 'Ladies, I thank you for stating your views so forthrightly, champion stuff. I will mull over the question in the course of the next few days and issue my decision by the end of the week. But right now, do excuse me.'

Liezel stood up, patting her wispy brown hair, Graça yapping at her ankles, 'Well, I think I've made my case quite strongly. I can't imagine what else there is to think about.'

Precious rose more slowly, as if the debate had drained her of her nervous energy. She did not look at me or say anything as she bent to pick up the tea tray.

*

Seven hours later I am standing with my toes over the edge of the bridge that lies in no man's land between Zambia and Zimbabwe, the thunderous noise of the Victoria Falls crashing behind me, the mighty Zambezi River roiling over the gleaming rocks below. Both banks of the river are covered in thick green foliage moistened by the constant spray propelled upwards by the rapidly moving water squeezing through the Batoka Gorge in white, foam-topped swirls. The sunrays here are different, slanting into an almost sunset, refracted through vibrating water droplets, which form a perennial rainbow.

My ankles are bound together with a towel-covered bolster cushioned between them; around my waist, a harness is attached to hoist me back up to the bridge afterwards, but now I am waiting for the freefall.

I turn to my son and wave into his phone as he endeavours to catch it all on video.

'5-4-3-2-1-BUNGEEEEEEEEEEEE!'

And I am falling through the sky, chest pushed outwards, surrendering to fatal gravity, my head seems severed from my plummeting body, the river is rushing up to meet me, sending its emissaries to moisten my cheeks like rain emanating from the ground instead of the sky. I plunge one hundred and eleven metres until suddenly there is a gentle yank and I swing, I swing, I swing, saved by the bungee cord just before it is too late, adrenaline roaring in my ears louder than the pounding tonnes of tumbling water.

Fragments from this morning's conversation splash through my head. Lucky, lacking Precious – with that desperate urgency to acquire more – is right! It is difficult if not impossible to maintain continuous evaporation without condensation. My waist harness is secured to the recovery line and they begin to winch me upwards, back to the catwalk, but I keep looking down into the fulminating waters below. Most of us are subject to the force of gravity. But equilibrium is maintained through balance.

Wiser not to rock the boat?

My son is waiting for me, brandishing his cellphone with the complete video. His teeth, unlike mine, are still naturally white and he is wearing a big grin, 'What goes down must come up.'

'Maybe,' I say, noncommittally, 'but for normal people, it's the other way round.'

51

The Initiation

Raisedon Baya

My first sexual encounter was nowhere near the mind blowing experience friends had told me it would be. It was not like anything I had read in books either. To be honest, it was a near disaster. All my friends had lost their innocence many years back and one of them, Tiza, already had a small family of his own at twenty-two, though he was struggling to look after it. It was only after the encounter that I realised my friends had lied to me, and that, perhaps, I should have taken their advice with a pinch of salt.

'If you haven't had sex then you haven't lived and have no idea what pleasure means,' Bigger told me one day after I had confessed my innocence to him. We were at the back of his mother's house lifting weights under the cool shade of a mango tree that his mother had been threatening to pull down for years. The tree protected us from the unfriendly glare of the sun. It was barren and, throughout its life, it had given Bigger's family nothing but shade; the reason Bigger's mother wanted to uproot it.

Bigger was not the first to tell me about the pleasure of sex. Mehluli and Tiza had told me the same thing; Mehluli even going to the extent of suggesting setting me up with a prostitute.

'Rush, if you're having difficulties getting a girl to initiate you into the world of pleasure, I can arrange an experienced woman for you,' he had said with a mischievous grin on his face. 'But this woman will cost you,' he added.

'You mean a prostitute?' I asked.

'They are now called pleasure givers,' he said, the grin on his face becoming a full-blown smile.

But it was Bigger's words that had the most effect on me. 'You're not a real man unless you hear the soft moaning of a woman under your belly, Rushmore,' he said as he handed me a big green towel that I used to mop away the rivers of sweat snaking down my neck and back. Bigger had stolen the towel at a city hotel after staying there for one night with a prostitute.

'Sex is not everything, besides I am going to have plenty once I get married,' I said to Bigger, the towel still in my hands. Bigger ignored me as he raised his weights, twisting his face in obvious pain.

Bigger loved weightlifting. He was obsessed with his physique. 'Women love a man with a good body,' he always preached to anyone who cared to listen. After the closure of the community youth centre, Bigger had waited two weeks before stealing the gym equipment and setting up his own backyard gym. His gym was nothing fancy. A few weights, two improvised bench presses, a Trojan exercise bicycle, a pair of dumbbells and some skipping ropes. And because the gym was now in his backyard, Bigger's home suddenly became a favourite hangout for our gang. It was here that we now came to whip our bodies into shape.

'So you're going to wait for marriage, heh?' Bigger asked and, before I could respond, he started laughing. The way he laughed made me want to lose my innocence that instant, right under that cool shade in his backyard. His laugh made me feel like the dumbest twenty-four-year-old alive. No. I didn't want to wait for marriage. I didn't even want to wait a day or two. I wanted to be a man that day, that moment. I was desperate to experience the pleasures Bigger and the others were always bragging about. The pleasures only women could give. I would wait for months before it happened and, by then, I was almost exploding with anxiety.

The day it happened I was so eager to become a man – to join my friends at the table of real men. The young woman who initiated me was no stranger. She was popular in the township. I later learnt she was no stranger to sex either. Her name was Muhle and she lived a few streets from ours.

Muhle was the only coloured girl who lived in the township. Her mother had brought her from South Africa and dumped her, and a brother from another father, with her grandmother. Muhle's brother,

Red Eyes, was not like her, he was dark. Almost charcoal black. His head was always completely shaved, displaying the ugly scars that he got from a violent street fight which nearly cost him his life. Red Eyes was a well-known gangster who spent most of his time behind bars and, if he was not behind bars, he was terrorising people, trying to drown himself in beer, or threatening to kill someone.

Muhle had small breasts and stuffed her bra with cotton wool to enhance their size. Her long shiny hair was tied into a neat bun at the back of her head. When she pulled her yellow and green dress over her head and unfastened her black bra, I nearly giggled as the cotton wool tumbled to the floor.

After removing her clothes she lay on the bed – a bed that Bigger had charged me five dollars to use for the afternoon. She lay on the bed with her eyes closed, as if she didn't want to see me or what Bigger's room looked like.

Naked, her body looked smooth and creamy. A few wiry hairs grew from her armpits and womanhood. Being the first time I had seen a naked woman, my mind went on overdrive. We didn't talk about what was about to happen. We were both afraid words would take away the magic of the moment.

'Come and hold me,' she whispered, making room for me on the single bed. I moved closer, kicking my trousers away. Her body was warm, triggering a series of explosions inside me. I remember seeing rainbows inside my head. Then it was over. I was lost. I didn't know what to do next. Muhle quickly realised what had happened and managed to mask her disappointment.

'Was this your first time?'

I nodded, embarrassed.

'Don't worry. Most men start the way you did. You'll learn to control yourself. I know next time you will do better,' she said, pulling herself away from me, and out of the bed. Unfortunately, there was to be no next time with her as I woke up a few days later with a greenish discharge. My manhood was on fire.

After a nightmarish week I sought medical help. By then I was telling myself I was a dead man. Dead man walking. In that week I don't know how many times I cursed Muhle. A nurse took me to an empty room where she ordered me to take off my trousers and underwear. Seeing my reluctance she told me, impatiently, that she had seen bigger and better men in the nude before.

'What's your name?' she asked.

'Rushmore.'

'Listen, Rushmore, I don't have the whole day here. Please take off your trousers and underwear and let me do my job.' Before I could respond she yanked open my trousers, pulled down my underwear, grabbed my penis in her gloved hands and proceeded to search for STI symptoms.

'Have you ever heard about condoms?'

'Yes.'

'Have you ever used one?'

'Yes,' I lied. She didn't seem to notice or even care.

'You should always use condoms. Sex is now a dangerous activity, especially for young people like you. People are losing their lives after two minutes of sex. And, believe me, sex is not worth dying for,' she said as she finished her inspection. She went out of the room and came back to inject my left buttock before giving me a packet of antibiotics.

'On your way out please pick up some condoms at the reception. They are free and meant to protect you,' she said, removing her gloves.

On my way out I didn't take the condoms, I cursed Bigger, Mehluli and Tiza. The initiation was their idea. They had said it would be the sweetest experience of my life. Instead it was turning out to be a nightmare. I cursed Muhle too. More than once.

The injection and pills from the clinic did not seem to help much. The pain continued. It was as if an army of ants had invaded my manhood and were competing to see which one had the best bite. Unable to bear the pain anymore I consulted a herbalist who operated from the open market, emkambo, near the municipality-owned beer hall, hoping to speed up the healing process.

The herbalist lived right on the outskirts of the city, in a squatter camp. He only came to the market for business. Consultations with him were done inside a black plastic shack where a few animal skins and bottled herbs were on display. The shack had an overpowering smell that was difficult to pin down. The herbalist's hair was white and he wore a wooden earing in one ear. After I explained my problem, the old man gave me a concoction to drink at home. He promised that I would be running and indulging again within a couple of days. He made my troubles sound minor, like my skin had just been scratched. The herbalist gave me a naughty smile and reassured me that what was happening was part of growing up. Nature taking its course. 'Egwazayo ibonakala ngamanxeba, mfana.'

He patted my back as I left his smelly shack. A fighting bull is identified by its scars. I was a bull now. Scarred and frightened.

The pain from the injection was nothing compared to the bitterness of the old man's medicine. The dark concoction was poison! A mouthful of it left a burning sensation right through to my intestines. Drinking it was as good as drinking acid. The only difference was that it didn't kill me. The herbalist's instructions were clear. One mouthful three times a day: morning, afternoon and evening. However, one evening, when the pain between my legs was too much to bear, I drank half the bottle and it upset my bowels so much that it had me running to the toilet for three full days.

The boys greeted the news of my initiation and infection with song and dance. A fighting bull is identified by its scars. The same words the herbalist had whispered to me. A man had been born. And so a mini-celebration to welcome me into the world of real men was hastily arranged. Bigger, Mehluli and Tiza took me braaing behind the old butchery at Fusini shopping centre. They bought a crate of beer and took turns to pour some of the contents on my head. It was like a birthday celebration. Or a graduation ceremony. Maybe it was both; a new birth and a graduation of some sort. I had moved from boyhood to manhood.

'You're now a real man, Rush,' the boys shouted, excited on my behalf.

Muhle came looking for me a few days later. She was still wearing the same yellow and green dress. Her hair was not tied up anymore. It fell all over her face.

'Did you tell your friends I gave you an STI?' There was venom in her voice. Her eyes were balls of fire.

'You should have warned me. At least I would have protected myself,' I shot back.

'It's not my fault you didn't wear a condom. And why didn't you come to me first? Now your friends are going about telling everyone that I'm rotten.'

'I'm sorry.'

'Imagine if I were to go about telling everyone that you're a thirty-second guy.'

I laughed. There was nothing else to do. It was an uneasy laugh. Dry and artificial.

'What's funny?' she asked, her hands now on her hips.

'So you're worried everyone will get to know you've an STI? Is that what is bothering you?

'No. What is worrying me is everyone knowing I slept with a loser like you.'

Words are like bullets. They can kill. Her words were bitterer than the poison I had been drinking all week. More painful than the STI she gave me. *Thirty-second loser! Me, a loser?* I had a mind to give her a thorough beating right there, but then the thought of her brother, Red Eyes, coming after me made me push the idea out of my mind. Perhaps she was right. I was a loser.

A Murder of Crows

Donna Kirstein

An ambush of widows or a grief of widows. The collective grouping of women who descend upon or lie in wait for the unsuspecting victim.

*

The crows here are black. Not white and black like back home. They congregate in parliamentary groups in the parks, scavenging leftovers from office workers at lunch. They pick apart the roadkill. Once I watched them tear apart a dead squirrel: ripping away red slivers of furred flesh. When they gather together, bickering over the scraps, they remind me of the ambush of widows at your funeral. It was October hot in Harare, with a tension and heat piling up against each other. The grass crackling under the weight of all your friends.

*

A spectre of ghosts, a fright, a fraid: ghosts haunt the living, occupying the space between life and death.

*

Sometimes in the dark you come back to me. I'm lying curled up between charity shop sheets. My side is throbbing. It's a form of haunting. It's gone one. Outside the changing seasons beat their pulse against the sash windows and the street is quiet. Autumn has crept in while I wasn't watching. As usual when I wake I know you are there in the room with me. The others in the house are quiet. If I hold my breath I can almost hear their soft snoring and sleep shifting against their mattresses. Sometimes there is just the noise of fucking and two people

58

going into it again and again and I know you are near. Occasionally I have to concentrate and focus; other times, like tonight, you just appear.

*

A murder of crows: there was a time when it was thought that crows were an omen of death. Certain folktales say that a group of crows will gather to decide on another crow's punishment and death.

*

Summer in England isn't what I thought it would be. I sit and watch the families at the park on my days off while the black-cloaked crows wait camouflaged in the trees.

It's been a while but I have finally stopped starting at the sound of your voice on the bus. I'm not jumping at shadows. For an impossible season I thought I saw you everywhere. The heat doesn't build up here like it did before, back when I was with you. The temperature's rising: the light here is not as sharp, it diffuses the angles, softening edges. I'm slowly starting to forget how the shadows would shorten and disappear at noon.

*

A moat of murderers: a crow, a fear of murderers, the noun doesn't seem definite, perhaps that is enough.

*

Sometimes I go to sleep and am woken in the night by the chill of winter as it twists its fingers around my wrists. I can feel your fingers, the calluses on your palms tightening around my neck. I can feel your warm breath against my skin, damp. In the dark I can hold my hands out and push and again you don't stop. You never stopped. I push against the fullness of your chest and can feel the wiry nest of your hair. I can push through, gently opening up your ribs until you cannot move again. If I concentrate I can push you further away, feel the warmth that drips against my skin. My child's blood, your blood, my blood: it's all the same now.

Soon I will have been here for longer than I was with you. Soon I will have finished remaking me. I am. Seagulls wake me in the morning. You wouldn't have liked that; you preferred the neighbour's cockerel strutting against the dawn.

*

A flight of migrants: the movement between places and states of mind, requiring an action that must be taken.

*

As the plane lands and we disembark, I focus on remembering who I am. Reminding myself that it's too late to go back. Your widows would be waiting and I was not going to surrender to that again. At the end of the queue the black-capped customs officials wait. Pushing away the phantom cramps in my side I step forward, presenting my papers. I am: I know my name again. No children. No family.

*

A shiver of sharks: the reaction when encountering a deadly focused animal.

*

My passport caused another argument. Why would I need a passport, and a British visa? You didn't understand why I wanted to visit my cousin. I might be able to persuade her to help with the child. The hospitals there would be better placed to treat him. How could you not understand that? How could you despise him already? It wasn't your fault. We argued. You threw things. And when you stopped the world had changed.

*

A squad of beaters: working together to re-establish the status quo, united and militaristic in focus.

*

After the second doctor's appointment you demanded answers. Who was he? I needed to do something. All your other children were well. It was because I smoked. It didn't matter that I had given up smoking when we were married. I had broken the future.

*

An annoyance of neighbours: the feelings invoked by the collective activities of neighbours.

*

The neighbour's cockerel wakes me. Every damn morning it wakes me and it's all I can do to keep myself from finding and strangling it. Today, it didn't crow or squawk or do whatever the fuck it thinks it's doing. I cannot believe it. There is another power cut but it doesn't matter because the bird is quiet. It seems too good to be true. It is. The women are gossiping at the fence. They don't like me. I told you but you laughed and said it was just because I was new; I was your new wife and your favourite. The others lived out and worked your lands. We would visit soon enough you said. Until then I should make more of an effort.

I hide the bruise on my arm; I wouldn't want them to talk. I don't want you to think I'm not making an effort. Wood smoke and dust. The air seems coated with diesel fumes and smoke. Dust is normally invisible but today as the particles hover in mid-air the winter light snags against them at an angle and I can see the dust motes dancing around my face. By the end of the day I knew for sure, we were having a child. By the next morning we had agreed that I should resign and stay home: to make the house ready for when the boy comes.

*

An eloquence of lawyers: the charming, strong-willed and well-spoken, against which there is no successful defence.

*

I never thought I was one of those women. I know you love me. You won me over with your courting, your persistence. You promised me the world, we went out dancing, you had friends who loaned us hotel rooms, you brought me roses. You were thoroughly modern, savvy and charming. You had connections, you laughed at my earnest political thoughts. You would take me to meet the real movers and shakers. You promised. The votes would happen again and again and you knew how important the answers were. From the start, you could predict with unerring accuracy the results, what would happen. But still we went together to make our mark. The men there nodding their heads so slightly at us with our blue-tipped fingers. The queue wound around the corner long into the day.

*

A promise of tomorrows: the possibility contained within an unattainable time.

*

I flushed with pride when you first took me back to your house. I was too modern for them. You grinned down at me. Your polished teeth glistened with the extra-whitening. We drove in and out in the smooth coolness of your new Mercedes. The neighbours whispered at the gates. You told me about your other wives, but I was the one for you. You sent your driver to collect me from work, encouraging me to resign, to move in with you. You stopped by at the busiest times to whisk me off for lunch or tea. My co-workers at the salon gushed and giggled whenever the Mercedes pulled up outside.

*

A string of pearls: the rope that binds elements together.

*

I was at work when we first met, outside smoking a Marlboro. You stood near me in your uncreased grey polyester suit. We flirted. You didn't like women who smoked. I thought you were joking. Your driver waited for you under the jacaranda tree; purple blossoms filled the air and stained the street. A drunken bee crawled out of a petal as we flirted. It crawled around in circles, dopey and light-headed from the pollen. You stepped forwards and crushed it under your crocodile skin boots.

Sunset Sketch

Christopher Mlalazi

Without warning, a group of women, skirts flying, exploded from around the corner of the bottle store, two policemen hot on their heels. It was too late for Muzi, Nehemiah and Sugar. They froze against the wall, faces expressionless, their eyes on the unholy chase. The woman who led the flight was Sugar's wife. She sold boiled groundnuts, eggs and cigarettes at the bottle store entrance to try to make ends meet for their family.

Night was rapidly crowding in and, to the west, a brilliant tint of gold and red stained the horizon, the final flare up before darkness blanketed Emakhandeni Township and the city of Bulawayo.

The women raced past them, feet pounding, and fled deeper into the township. The policemen suddenly gave up the chase. Nehemiah watched them turn around and walk back towards them. With their baton sticks and heavy boots, they looked formidable, as if they could batter down concrete walls with their bare fists. 'Don't panic guys,' he whispered between his teeth.

Sugar, tall and reed thin, slinked to Nehemiah's far side, away from the view of the policemen, who were eyeing them suspiciously. He was drunk, and his lower lip hung loosely.

'The people at church are going to be impressed by your new song tomorrow,' Nehemiah said to Muzi, unnecessarily loud. He had a strikingly handsome face that was carried arrogantly, chin high.

'You are right,' Muzi agreed, nodding his head, silently praying that the approaching policemen would not search them. He was dressed in a red dragon shirt, black tracksuit bottoms with a single white stripe

63

and white Super Pros. 'We must try to get a radio interview for more publicity,' he continued.

The two policemen walked past. One of them was rapping his baton stick against the wall, as if in anticipation of seeing it work somewhere. 'They think we are playing,' the policeman was muttering. 'They need beating very hard!' The policemen disappeared around the building.

Nehemiah burst out laughing, pointing at Sugar.

'Look at you,' he said. 'You nearly wet your trousers, yet you are not drinking like us! You mustn't be afraid of the police. They are your friends, not your enemy.'

'They are my enemy,' Sugar declared, his voice slurred. In his own peculiar way, he was right. Sugar was the township rogue, one of those fellows who seem not to be able to discriminate right from wrong, and are always in and out of jail for various petty crimes. 'You just talk talk talk, but you don't know cent.' He was looking at his wife, who stood a distance away at a street corner with a group of women, all forlorn looking, and waiting for the police to go so they could return and see what remained of their merchandise in front of the bottle store.

'That you sell mbanje?'

'You just fart,' Sugar replied. 'One day the cops will get you at your corner in town and you will shit yourself instead.'

'They will get your mother,' Nehemiah replied. He pointed at Sugar's wife, laughing. The group of women were now walking away, headed for home, probably having decided that home was better than police cells. 'Maputo Express.' He pumped his hands in the motion of a running athlete.

Muzi's eyes, in a moon shaped face, briefly lingered on the vivid stain on the horizon, its delicate beauty the cry of his heart at the ugliness that surrounded his life.

The wall they leaned against stank strongly of urine, but the three men ignored the smell, for they were used to it. They stood here every day at sunset to have a couple of beers to wrap up the day like a reed mat, before going to their homes.

Sugar abruptly changed subject. 'So you guys think you are clever huh? Hiding beers in your pockets. I see I should have told those two policemen about it.' He turned to Muzi, now smiling. 'For not telling on you, sir, buy me a beer too, so that I can drink it from my pocket like you shefs.' His body swayed drunkenly, like a stalk of elephant grass before a wind. He had just joined them from the beer garden where he had been drinking masese since noon, having knocked off early from his job as a pushcart operator in town.

'I doubt very much the trousers you are wearing still have a pocket remaining,' Nehemiah said. 'If you put your hand inside you touch balls, don't you?'

'Shut up you,' Sugar retorted. He wore a pair of old jeans, heavily patched at the knees.

'I would rather buy you a loaf of bread, my friend,' Muzi told Sugar, 'so when you get home you can have something to eat.' He took out a two dollar bond note from his pocket. 'Decide. Bread or nothing?'

A man was approaching in their direction along the wall, in each hand bulging carrier bags.

Sugar bent down and reached into his right sock. When he straightened, there was an okapi in his hand. He pulled its blade open with his teeth. Then, his lower lip clenched between his teeth, he screeched the blade against the wall. The approaching man suddenly turned around and hastily walked back the way he had come, casting fearful glances over his shoulder at Sugar.

'Futsek!' Sugar shouted. The man broke into a trot, carrier bags swinging, and disappeared around the corner.

Nehemiah laughed. Muzi shook his head at Sugar. He had recognised the man. It was Moyo, the pastor of the local SDA church. He hoped he had not been recognised; it would be so embarrassing if he met Moyo again, even if he did not go to his church, or any other church for that matter. Muzi was a born-free as far as religion was concerned, believing in waking up in the morning and pursuing instinct, although he swore in the good name of the Lord God whenever the road was not clear.

'When will you grow up, Sugar?' Muzi asked him. 'Insulting people you don't even know, like a mad man.'

'Maybe I am mad,' Sugar replied. He slashed at the air in front of him with the knife. 'This country is driving me mad!' He slashed again, as if slashing the belly of the country, then he snapped the okapi closed, and, with a flourish, bent down and returned it to his sock. Straightening, he held out his right hand at Muzi, palm open.

Christopher Mlalazi

'What is it going to be?' Muzi asked him. He drank from his beer bottle before putting it back in his pocket, making sure the tails of his shirt were covering it.

'The money,' Sugar said. 'You just promised me. Don't tell me you have forgotten so fast. Should I sharpen my knife on the wall again?'

'Futsek,' Muzi replied. 'You think your knife scares me?' He jabbed a finger at Sugar's thin chest. 'I told you I am buying you a loaf of bread, not alcohol. Now decide quickly before I change my mind, bastard.' He extended his ear towards Sugar's mouth.

'A loaf of bread, my bra,' Sugar replied politely, curtsying.

Muzi smiled, gave him the money and patted his shoulder. 'You are my friend,' he told him.

'And tomorrow morning come and clean up my car, boy,' Nehemiah said, chin held up. 'I have a good pair of shoes I want to throw away.' He lit a cigarette and flicked the matchstick away. 'Look at your shoes. You can afford to buy masese everyday at the beer garden, yet you can't think of buying yourself a pair of cheap decent shoes, or taking those you are wearing to a cobbler. Did you pick them up from a dry river bed by the way?'

Sugar's shoes looked as if they had seen centuries – they were grubby and torn at the front, exposing his toes and shreds of socks, as if they were laughing at the poor state of their wearer.

Muzi looked at the ground in embarrassment. His eyes flitted to the new Nike sneakers on Nehemiah's feet. He took out his beer and drank. Nehemiah did the same.

'I will come and clean your Benz, Minister of Finance,' Sugar said, chortling. He extended his hand towards Nehemiah's cigarette. 'Bring that cigarette, I want two pulls,' he demanded.

'Bring it?' Nehemiah asked, resting his left hand on his hip, his brow furrowed. 'This is not your wife's pot-hole, my boy.' He inhaled and exhaled a steady stream of smoke, looking at Sugar obliquely.

'Say, please can I have a cigarette,' Muzi advised Sugar.

'Can I please have a cigarette, shef?' Sugar repeated after Muzi, his eyes hooded.

'Good,' Nehemiah said. He pulled another cigarette from his pocket, lit it with his, and handed it to Sugar.

Sugar took the cigarette. 'Thanks,' he said. He drew on it and blew a steady stream of smoke at Nehemiah's face. 'Arsehole.'

Muzi found himself laughing.

Nehemiah just smiled, dangerously. 'You got me there,' he said. 'Don't worry. Laugh last, laugh the longest, is my motto.'

'Laugh first, laugh the longest, is my motto,' Sugar said, laughing loudly, his mouth opened wide, his body arched backwards with the effort, then he staggered away, still laughing.

Nehemiah and Muzi watched him reeling around the corner and out of view.

Nehemiah shook his head. 'You shouldn't have given him the money. Drunk as he is, he will fall against a shelf in the supermarket and break something valuable.'

'You are right.' Muzi agreed, worry on his face. 'In fact, I should have gone and bought the bread for him.'

Spinx, the local dog that was also a regular at the bottle store, limped past on its rounds. On the other side of the building was an open braai, and that was Spinx's destination. Spinx had fled his home a couple of years previously for a life on the streets when his master had been arrested for illegal gold possession. A drunk at the bottle store had once enticed Spinx with a piece of meat, then, for fun, masturbated the dog in front of a shocked crowd of drinkers.

'Who would believe that Sugar was once a school teacher?' Nehemiah said, smiling snakishly. 'And look at him now – even Spinx is better than him.'

Muzi shrugged his shoulders lamely in reply, feeling uncomfortable with the direction in which the conversation had now shifted – he didn't like gossiping, especially about friends. And his life wasn't so rosy either.

'I wonder what made him get fired from his teaching job,' Nehemiah continued. 'It must have been something pretty serious, because the Civil Service does not just fire you that easily.'

'He drinks too much,' Muzi replied, his voice low, hoping that Nehemiah would take the hint and change the topic.

But Nehemiah was not finished. 'It can't have been only alcohol,' his voice also lowered. 'I heard some guys say he was caught fondling the breasts of a Grade Six student.' His eyes were shining as he delivered the last piece of news.

'People say all kinds of things about other people's lives,' Muzi said. 'But I think it is the alcohol that was the root problem. He drinks far too much.'

'The alcohol is a family problem,' Nehemiah said. 'Why, only yesterday his wife went past very drunk – you were not here and I was standing alone. You should have seen her, my friend, she had pissed her skirt.' He shook his head. 'Poverty is not good, Muzi. Hear it from me. I am happy that God has been kind to me and my family can afford to sleep on a full stomach every day.'

Nehemiah was semi-literate, having only gone as far as Grade Five in primary school.

Muzi cracked the knuckles of his left hand nervously. Their conversation had taken a further wrong turning. Sometimes he and his wife slept on empty stomachs. And he had gone as far as Advanced Level at school, coming out with distinctions, but his parents had lacked the money to give him a university education.

There was a sudden commotion at the corner of the bottle store; now four police, three male and one female, appeared dragging a handcuffed person. They got nearer. Muzi opened his mouth in surprise. The handcuffed person was Sugar. A group of people, mostly kids, were following behind them, the kids chanting in loud excited voices, 'Thief! Thief! Thief!'

The group passed Muzi and Nehemiah, who made sure their bottles of beer were well out of sight in their pockets. Sugar's head was bowed and he did not look in their direction. Muzi stopped one of the chanting kids.

'What has he done, Delight?'

'He stole an ice cream in the supermarket and put it under his armpit, but it fell down at the security guard's feet at the door,' Delight replied in feverish excitement, then scooted after the group.

'See what I told you!' Nehemiah said to Muzi.

'And now he is going to need a fine.' Muzi almost wailed.

'Don't bother yourself about him. You were only trying to help when you gave him the two dollars, isn't it so? Sometimes I wonder why you associate with his kind, Muzi. Look at you. You are a famous and well-travelled mbube musician, and you should seek better people to make friends with. That guy is shit.'

Their beers were finished. Darkness had swelled over the township, but the tower lights peeping over the township roofs like sentinels had not yet come alight.

'Bring your bottle,' Nehemiah said. 'This is my round.'

Muzi gave it to him. 'Last round,' he said. 'I have something important to do before I go to sleep.' There was nothing important he needed to do in his lodging room. This was just an excuse to get away, for he had no more money – he had only had money for one beer.

'Sure,' Nehemiah replied. 'It's getting late. I don't like standing here at this hour. ' He turned around, opened his zip, the beer bottles held by their necks in one hand, and relieved himself against the wall.

Two children, a boy and a girl, who had been approaching, stood a safe distance away until Nehemiah was finished, after a noisy and abrasive fart.

Nehemiah did his zip up. 'It doesn't rain without thunder – mhh. And this wall stinks!' he remarked, then walked around the building.

'Muzi!' The boy, who was not more than twelve years old, said when the children drew abreast of him.

'Irvine and Buhle, you must only come to the shops early, it's not nice here after sunset.'

'We like it at this hour, just like you,' the boy replied as they went past.

Muzi did not reply, but just shook his head and looked at the nearest tower light as it slowly and magically flared into an orange glow. Other lights across the township followed.

The shadows at the back of the bottle store melted away, revealing more men leaning against the length of the wall, all drinking alcohol, and talking animatedly.

'Hello Muzi,' a voice greeted him. It was Chemist, who was screwing the bottom of an unlit candle into the narrow mouth of an empty cooking oil bottle.

'Chemist. How's it going, my boss?'

'The game is starting now,' Chemist replied. 'Still don't want to play? You could make easy money, no sweat, and buy yourself nice things. Life needs brains these days.'

'No thank you. The police have just passed by, watch out.'

Chemist was a gambler who played cards by candlelight every night under the barren mango tree behind the bottle store.

'Don't worry yourself about the police. At night they don't bother us. Anyway, what can baton-stick carrying policemen do to us? We are not women like that fuck Sugar who stole an ice cream, a thing for children.' He spat. 'He should steal money like a man.' He walked away towards the mango tree, where a dangerous looking dark huddle of men were already waiting for him.

Nehemiah came back with the two beers. He handed one to Muzi, and they opened them with their teeth. They sipped the cold beer.

'It's so difficult to sit in the house at this time of the day,' Nehemiah said, lighting a cigarette. Muzi did not smoke. 'I don't know why.' He looked up and blew smoke. Wide-spaced stars winked dully in the sky, their light overshadowed by the tower lights.

'Maybe it's because our houses are so empty,' Muzi replied, and immediately regretted it. But he decided to continue. 'In the eastern suburbs you hardly see a soul outside at this hour – they have everything in their houses.'

'No, it's not that. My house is not empty, and you know that very well. I have everything, TV, DVD, Wi-Fi to log in to that crap called Facebook, beer in the fridge, but here I am leaning against a piss-stinking wall at the bottle store. I think it's something else, something hard to describe.'

'Maybe the drama of the bottle store.'

'Could be that. One would think that this place has us bewitched. Muzi, let's go buddy, the bottle store is closing now.'

All around, men were detaching themselves from the wall and heading away, some homewards, some to shebeens to continue boozing, and, of course, some to commit crime somewhere, now that alcohol had given them the courage.

Nehemiah and Muzi also walked away, their beers now held in their hands openly, but their eyes alert for police. They came to the street corner where they always parted and stopped, their shadows elongated at an angle on the tarred road from a nearby tower light.

'We have a show at Luveve Cocktail Bar tomorrow evening,' Muzi said. 'It's five dollars to get inside, but let me give you a complimentary ticket. I have a few for friends.'

He took out his wallet, extracted a ticket and handed it to Nehemiah. Muzi was the lead vocalist for Abakhwenyana Ensemble.

Nehemiah took the ticket and put it into the breast pocket of his shirt without looking at it.

'What time is the show?' he asked.

'7 pm.'

'I'll come, then after your show we can drive to town and have a good time. There is a late night fashion show at the Rainbow Hotel that I don't want to miss. The admission is twenty bucks.'

'Twenty dollars!'

'Don't worry, it's only bond notes. And I will pay for you. I know you cannot afford it, but what are friends for? I would rather have your company than anybody else's; after all, girls like your face, you are always on the TV and radio, and we might manage to have some fun with a few.'

'If you can afford it, I can't refuse the offer.'

'Okay, so see you tomorrow then, and nice sex at home.'

Muzi laughed, they parted and went in different directions towards their dwellings. They stayed three streets apart.

Muzi whistled softly the tune of their latest song, the one they had been rehearsing the whole day at Emakhandeni Hall, a song that bemoaned ever-soaring prices, bad governance and abject poverty. A dog barked viciously at him from behind a fence, as if warning him that whistling the song might portend a calamity with the authorities. He feinted with his right hand towards a half brick on the ground. The dog yelped and darted away even before he could straighten up, its tail between its legs.

Muzi continued with his song, now singing in a low voice:

They shall attempt to silence us
But who can stifle an infant's cry
When its lips crave to suck?
They shall attempt to silence life
But who can stifle a child's cry
When there is no sign in the sky
That things will ever change...

The Library of the Dead

T.L. Huchu

No place left to run. The world is but a globe; circle it enough times and you return to where you started, over and over, no matter how hard you try for lift-off. That is how I find myself with her (the book) clutched to my breast on the roof of Karigamombe Centre in Harare. The city is bathed in light and the pregnant moon squats over everything, giving birth to a new season.

The dark figure with a familiar limp approaches, gun in hand. He is my father.

'Return the book and all will be forgiven,' he calls out in a tired voice. 'Come back to us. We can start afresh. You really think you're the first person to have ever felt this way?'

They sent him after me when I stole the book. I hid in the slums of Nairobi and he found me, I fled from Paris to Rome, through London and then across the marshes of the Amazon, with nothing but a backpack with a few clothes and her (the book). We fought in Bogota, nearly drowned off the coast of Guyana, and in Mexico City we danced with silver knives flashing sparks amidst the dense throng of the Day of the Dead.

Each time I fled and he found me. So I came back here, to end it all.

'What other choice do I have?' I shout out, angry, my words shrapnel from an explosive device.

'To surrender. The head librarian has given his word, you will not be harmed.' In the moonlight, the barrel of his .45 Magnum almost looks beautiful.

I back away onto the ledge. He steps nearer.

'Son, this is madness.' I hear the grief in his voice, but my choice is made. There is another way.

She speaks to me through my fingertips on her (the book's) leather cover. 'It's okay. Give me up. Let me return to that dungeon, so you can be free,' she says. Never. I feel the cool breeze of the night air as it sweeps the thoroughfares, glancing off steel and glass and concrete, caressing my warm skin. I smile. I choose to fall—

*

When I was fifteen, Baba withdrew me from Oriel where I was doing my form four and found me a job. You know the Heroes Acre in the west of Harare as you go towards Norton? Before that, I'd only ever seen it on TV on national holidays. Baba wore a black dovetail suit and black tie, complete with top hat, like an undertaker. The Vaseline on his dark skin made him appear as if he was a polished wooden sculpture. His stiff, deliberate movements were those of an automaton and, when I was younger, my friends and I took to imitating him.

We passed through Barbours on First Street, where he bought me a similar outfit. I remember driving through the packed streets lined with vendors in our blue Ford Anglia. The chrome glistened in the mid-morning sun. On empty squares, chamupupiri picked up dust, leaves and litter, twirling them round like ballerinas. I watched it all, my arm hanging out the window as we cruised along the A5.

'You will tell no one of the things you will see when we get to where we are going. You hear me?' Baba said, his hands 10 and 2 on the steering wheel.

'Okay.'

'Not even your mother.'

'Cool.'

Baba reached into his breast pocket with his right hand, pulled out a pack of Kingsgate, opened it and bit one out with his teeth. He returned the packet, took out a lighter and lit up. He was a 20-a-day man. This is the scent I knew him by, as if the tobacco had somehow embedded itself into his very being.

*

The soldier who stood guard at the Heroes Acre waved us through. Baba favoured him with the slight tip of his head. We parked and walked over to the monument. I felt awkward in my new outfit. Sure the fabric was smooth, but I was not used to suits and the like. It made me feel rather old. The three golden soldiers on the Tomb of the Unknown Soldier maintained their eternal guard as we ascended the black granite steps. An old wreath lay at their feet. I was struck by their strength and beauty, two men and a woman frozen forever in time.

'Tread lightly, this is sacred ground,' my father said.

I didn't know what to answer.

We ascended the stairs and Baba stopped and bowed at the monument. We walked around it to the black wall with a coat of arms atop it. In front of the bricks, Baba pressed one near his chest, then skipped two right, pressed another and then he stood on his toes and pressed another. I leapt back with fright as the stones on the wall groaned and pulled back to reveal a doorway 3 by 6 feet high. We walked into the darkness and the stones rearranged themselves into a solid wall behind us. Baba clapped his hands and lights came on revealing a long corridor of black granite. Along the corridor were pictures of old men and women.

'What is this place?' I asked.

'Few people know of it,' was his reply.

A solid wooden door opened at the end of the corridor and we walked into a large circular room illuminated by numerous candles whose flickering flames cast long shadows swaying on the walls. There was a wooden desk at the front, and behind it sat a silver-haired man in white overalls. Baba crouched and clapped his hands in the old way, and I went down to join him, clapping mine too.

'This is your boy?' the man asked.

'He is.'

'A bit young… but he will do, I suppose,' the man said, standing up. 'Come with me, child.'

I remained where I was until Baba nudged me, saying, 'Go with the head librarian.' My legs were shaky when I stood up, and I went round the table. The old man waved my father away and I watched him walk out, the sound of his footsteps echoing along the long corridor.

The head librarian led me into a large room carved in the hill behind the monument, which we were directly underneath. We wound up in a chamber that was full of shelves upon shelves of books as far as the eye could see. It smelled ancient, musty and meaty.

'What is this place?' I asked.

'Talkers often don't last long here,' he said, with a chuckle that echoed through the room. 'Welcome to the Library of the Dead.'

I heard a faint applause, followed by some murmuring. Voices rose up from dark corners, echoing on the stone walls.

'Shh,' he said. 'The books, you see, they like to talk. But this is a library and talking is forbidden.'

The shelf nearest me sagged under the weight of books, all with leather binding of black or varying shades of brown. It was cold in the room, but I was warm in my suit.

'The Great Zimbabwe Empire was built by kings under the instructions of the Memorykeepers. You have heard of them, no? Of course not. It is an old – for lack of a better word – guild that has been there for as long as our people have been around. The Memorykeepers' task is to remember everything. Among them were great architects, stonemasons, farmers, storytellers, healers, warriors and wizards, but their key task was to keep the Dark at bay, which they did, for centuries.' He paused and looked at me to see I was taking everything in. 'When the English came, we were in the Hundredth War against the Dark. Unable to hold two fronts, the Memorykeepers ceded to man, so they could continue their battle against the Dark. A few dissented, you know them as Nehanda, Kaguvi and Chaminuka; they are heroes to you and you are taught this in school, but the true heroes, the ones you know nothing about, are the ones who kept to their core task, which is holding off the Dark, for the sake of all mankind.'

'That's pretty cool, I suppose,' I said. He shot me a look.

'But now there are fewer Memorykeepers than at any stage in the past and they cannot hold all the new knowledge that flows from the four corners of the world. Fewer every generation are born with the gift. So they created us, a suborder; we do not have their magical gifts, but what we do is to hold the knowledge that they cannot.'

*

And so I was inducted as an assistant in the Library of the Dead. I spent my apprenticeship directly under the head librarian, who for all his silver hair was sharp and nimble. The books we held did not have titles, only names. You got used to the noise in the place, the voices chatting, the sobbing in dark corners, the arguing, revolutionary songs and lullabies. It was seldom quiet in the library, except for when the head librarian was in. Only he could command the books to hush. Most of the time, it felt like a crowded marketplace.

Our clients who came after dark were usually sombre-looking men and women who barked orders at us with some disdain.

'Get me *Petros Molaicho*! I asked for *Garande* not *Grange*!

Tafadzwa Munengami! *Border Gezi* is useless, make mine *Manyika*! *David Moore*! *Chatonga Ponayi*, urgently!

Quickly, *Lionel Cripps*! I must have that book!

Reserve *Chipanga* for me!'

And my job was to run through the maze of books with my cart and get whatever it was the patrons wanted. My feet often ached and few of those people ever said thanks. But my job was to hand over the books. I was strictly forbidden from reading them.

*

Half a year into the job, I fell in love with her (the book). I'd learnt to ignore the books that called out to me, because they were all so demanding and it was hard to meet all their needs at once. The older ones that were not read would ask me to take them off the shelf, open them up for just a minute so they could breathe the fresh air and let the candlelight that lit our hall caress their pages. Crippled books that were broken from bad handling begged for massages to their spines or to be put out of their misery.

It was her (the book's) voice, amidst all that noise, that called to me. How to describe it: set the scene – I was mopping the floors early one morning when I heard it, breathy like wind caught in the leaves of a mango tree, crackling like twigs in a low flame, gentle and soft like cotton wool. It reminded me of Scarlett Johansson.

'Hello... is anyone there... it's so cold in here.'

She wasn't louder than any of the other books. Her (the book's) voice came under the noise, reaching out to touch my cloak. I found her (the book) in the Y shelf, in the corner, right at the bottom and retrieved her (the book).

'I'm here,' I said.

'Oh, thank you. It's been such a long time since I've been touched.'

'Sorry, I guess.'

'Can you put me under a candle, so I can feel its warmth just for a second? Please. Just for one moment.'

Her (the book's) cover felt soft and supple as if I was holding a young baby. I oiled her (the book) and placed her (the book) under a flickering candle. She cooed, maybe remembering what it was once like to sit under the sun.

'What's your name?' she asked.

'Anotenda,' I said.

'I'm *Yeukai*,' she replied.

I wasn't fond of books in school. Dead wood, black and white ink. But these books; they say the voice is closer to the essence of a person than the written word, that speech is purer, proximal to the soul. And how she talked. Her (the book's) voice touching every empty crevice of my being.

The head librarian had warned me about growing attached to any of the books. They were but useful tools. There was no time for favouritism. But I found myself drawn to her (the book) over and over. I secretly read her (the book's) pages, her (the book's) incomplete story, since she was made at sixteen, keeping her (the book) trapped in an incomplete tale, one that held so much promise, but was never realised. I snuck out with her (the book), from time to time, hidden under my jacket, pressed close to my flesh, going to parks, cafes, on kombis, to malls and in my room, under my pillow when I slept at night.

*

After my first year, the head librarian told me he was satisfied with my progress. He was making a new book and wanted me to assist in the process. There was a wrought iron door at the end of the library. He took out a large key, which clanged as he undid the lock, opened the door and let us in. We walked down steep spiral stairs lit by oil torches, descending deep into the bowels of the earth until we wound up in a large domed room with murals of cherubim and seraphim all over it. In the centre of the room lay a corpse on a gurney. I was startled and recoiled.

'Young man, do not be afraid,' the librarian said, 'we will make a book today.'

There was a large stainless steel cupboard against the left wall and he led me to it. We retrieved surgical scrubs, masks and gloves. As we dressed, the head librarian chanted, 'Muzuva nemumvura/ murimi anosimira achidiridza neziya/ zvake uyo akatsungarara/ achidyara achitimbira achiriritira/ gohwo riri kure…' The words were dizzying and, once he started reciting, he never stopped. His instructions to me were passed through gestures as he pointed to one thing or the other. He made me lay out on a metal trolley the sharp tools, cutters and hammers, along with cloths, sponges and bottles of acrid chemicals. We took all these things to the corpse.

'Nyama yakava izwi' – the flesh was made word.

It was in this room that important people and select ordinary folks from all walks of life were brought after their deaths. The librarian took a scalpel from the trolley, pressed it on the corpse's forehead, just below the hairline, and made an incision. Dark red blood oozed out, just a little.

We flayed the corpse; the skin would make the cover of the book. The hair would be woven into fibres to stitch the book together and the glue to bind it would be made from the bones. The entrails, we emptied into a large yellow bin that kicked up an overwhelming stench. We separated the muscles and organs, the heart and the brain and the liver. It was hard work and I sweated under my scrubs. My feet and back ached, but the librarian who was an older man showed no discomfort, just an intense concentration that never once faltered, even as I dabbed his brow with a sponge, as if he were a surgeon at work.

When all the components of the man were separated and placed onto the tables in the far corner, blood collected in buckets, the head librarian turned to me.

'We will peel these parts into paper thin slices, I will show you how. The blood will be the ink. This process can take a while, so we must be patient,' he said.

For days, we worked, bit by bit, creating the book from every part of the man. We used various mysterious chemicals to transform the flesh into pages. When the book was ready, we dipped it into the bucket of blood, prevented from congealing by our anticoagulants. The blood would soak into text and write the tale the soul told.

*

I helped make many books in my time at the Library of the Dead. Each fascinated me. When we were not making books, I cared for the ones on the shelves, repaired holes rats had gnawed, set traps for rats, oiled covers, catered to the patrons. There was little separation between my work and my life, because the head librarian had ordered my things brought from home and given me a little garret in the library. I lived here, ate here, studied for my GCSEs (from normal books) here, under his instructions.

But for all I did, she remained my one obsession, my true passion. The little free time I had, I spent in her (the book's) pages. Baba, who worked in another part of the library, came to see me and check on my progress from time to time, usually around dinner or lunch.

'I am told you are making good progress,' he said.

'It's weird dope here,' I replied.

'There's something I need to talk to you about.' He wore his grave daddy face and his voice lowered a fraction. 'You are a young man, it must be difficult for you to be cooped up here all the time. But this is an important job. I just want you to be very careful about the books. They can be tricksy, fill your head with notions, crazy things. These books are not normal books and you must treat them with caution. Only the Memorykeepers have the power to fully decipher them and to master them for their own ends. There is a clear separation between us, the makers and the custodians of the text, and them, the readers.'

'I hear you,' I said quietly.

I wondered if he knew about her (the book) and if this talk served as a warning. Maybe it did, or it was just part of my apprenticeship, advice from the master to his pupil. But I could not stop; there was something in our communion that spoke to the deepest parts of my being. That very night, I went to read her (the book).

She told me she was cold and lonely, seldom read and wanted to leave. 'To be put out of my misery,' as she put it. And our library had a great many books that sat lonely on shelves, year after year. I did the best I could for them, dusting them, rearranging them on shelves, feeling their gratitude for my touch. Even books that had once been read often, by many, sometimes found themselves suddenly out of favour, falling into disuse and solitude.

She was just an ordinary person who had been selected to join the library, because the Memorykeepers had to have knowledge of all things, great and small, but the truth is that they were mostly interested in the great. The longer I stayed in that library, the more I thought about my own purpose. I could be there and serve many books, the best I could, which was far from enough, or I could dedicate my life to the service of one, of her (the book), study her (the book) intensely, deeply, meaningfully and tie myself to her (the book) entirely.

'I will take you away into the world,' I said.

'Will you? Would you really do that for me – to risk everything?' she said in a small voice, as if trying not to let the hope it carried expand.

And that is how I fled the Library of the Dead on the midnight train to Bulawayo. I kept her (the book) under my shirt, her (the book's) cover touching my breast to keep her (the book) warm. There, I could feel her (the book) breathe. I told her (the book) of the vast savannah, silhouettes of trees under the Milky Way, the innumerable stars. In the morning we took the bus across the border to Joburg. And so my father's pursuit began. Each time I thought I'd found a town, a hamlet, a city where we could be alone together, he found us. But we ran, around the world, through bazaars in Istanbul, across the Arabian desert on the backs of camels, over the Tora Bora mountains, through crowded cities in Pakistan and India, favelas in South America. Each time I read her (the book) I fell into little cracks, parts of the story I had missed the last time, understood new meanings I'd not deciphered before.

But with each step I took deeper into her (the book) the world only grew smaller and smaller. Soon, there was nowhere left to hide.

*

—outstretched arm reaches out into the darkness towards me, but it is too far, my father cannot make the catch. Under the pregnant moon, the air slips away from my back like silken sheets. I clutch her (the book) to my heart and listen to the wind whisper Zezuru melodies to my descent.

I feel the world rush by, the chains of time slip away, each link broken. Together. I hold her (the book) tighter, my fingers digging into her (the book's) leather cover as if we are making sweet love under the street lights on a bed of hard concrete pavement, which gives not to my back as I lie down, bones breaking, skull shattering, my insides bursting into strawberry jam. Baba leans over the ledge, cursing the universe.

And then, the blood that flows from my shredded veins seeps into her (the book's) pages, finding little spaces on the yellow pages, the gaps between letters and paragraphs. Turning into Ls and Os and Vs and Es, the vowels and consonants that make us. Until nothing is left of the blankness, but a full unity, no margins or spaces or full stops. Just one complete perfect illegible book only we can read.

The Cure

Patricia Brickhill

It had been more than a decade when he walked back into her life. They'd never been more than casual friends but their paths crossed and their lives touched in the way that lives sometimes do. They'd frequented the same haunts, listened to the same live music, waved across the room at the same parties. She had always told him she loved the sound of his voice – she couldn't hear enough of it and it sent shivers of delight down her spine with its echoing bass tones.

She was seated at a table in the café with her children eating supper when he bellowed her name in joyful recognition. Turning, she smiled when she saw the owner of that familiar voice. He threw up his hands, dropping the Bon Marché bag he had been clutching seconds before. It fell with a loud thud but he didn't take any notice. Her chair scraped loudly on the stone floor as she hurriedly got to her feet. They hugged; he kissed her on one cheek then, haphazardly, awkwardly, on the other.

She felt overwhelmed by how very happy she was to see him. Subconsciously she had been searching for someone to link her to her previous life, the one that she had lost all those years ago but still missed so utterly. It seemed that he simply needed a friendly face, one with a purse full of change.

'I've come out and I only have a hundred dollar bill. I need five dollars for the taxi driver and he's outside waiting impatiently.'

Her head bowed and she opened the small green and black tapestry purse that hung around her neck and searched through the soiled dollar bills.

'I'm sure I have some.' She counted them one by one. 'Here.'

He grabbed them out of her hand and rushed out of the café. She looked up and realised her children had stopped their conversation mid-sentence to witness this spectacle.

'Wow! You actually know him. He is such an amazing musician.'

Smiling to herself, before she could answer that she had a real life once, he was back at her side. His lips parted in what might be recognised as a smile. He pressed her arm awkwardly against his thigh, as she had already sat back down.

'Are these your children?'

He greeted each one as if meeting them made him happier than he had ever been before. Then he turned to her as if they no longer existed.

'Thank you, my dear. I told the taxi driver to go to the Zuva garage or to Nando's to look for change but he refused. I will pay you back.'

'Oh don't worry; there's no need. I was glad to be able to help and I'm just so happy to see you again.'

'No. No. No – I insist. I will send your money over after I have bought something.'

He turned away and left them to look for an empty table. Later that evening the waiter appeared and held out his battered metal tray. On it were five grubby dollar bills, almost an exact replica of the ones she had given to her old friend earlier. As she stretched out her hand to take them she glanced over towards his table.

His face lit up when their eyes met and he smiled. 'Thank you,' she mouthed over the noise. He shook his hands in front of his face, 'No, thank YOU,' he mouthed back pointing first to himself and then to her with exaggerated emphasis.

The performances were underway and she glanced occasionally in his direction. She saw him order one beer after another. His head was bowed at times and then he would raise it as if he were speaking to someone on his right. But there was no one else at his table. She saw him get up to go to the bar. He left his Bon Marché packet on the table, a neat pile of books next to it as a sign of ownership. A young man standing nearby ignored the items on the table and pulled the chair out to sit down. A few minutes later her friend reappeared.

There was an angry exchange and then a loud slap, as her friend hit the young man. The tirade continued until he struck the young man again. He staggered back this time with the force and melted into the crowd.

The woman told her children what she had seen. Her oldest son went to speak to her friend. They spoke and then he returned to the table to speak to his mother.

'He said he wants me to buy him a beer.'

'Ask him if he wants some food. He has had several beers too many already.'

Her son returned to the other table and her friend gestured him to sit down. They spoke and she continued speaking to her other children. When her son came back he told his siblings it was time for them to go on stage and perform their set. She almost forgot about the earlier incident as she proudly watched them play, swaying to the music. Afterwards they went out to the beer garden so she could smoke. When they got up to go home, she decided she could not disappear without saying goodbye to her old friend. He cut a lonely figure now, sitting alone at his table, shunned by the other patrons.

She put her hand on his shoulder and squeezed it in a gesture of affection. He pulled her nearer.

'Everyone thinks I am mad,' he said, holding her uncomfortably close. 'Have you heard that? Everyone thinks I am mad but they don't know me.'

She was taken aback, but didn't know how to respond, so she was silent.

'I know things. I know you still loved him,' he continued. 'Divorce doesn't finish love. I found that out the hard way and now you know that as well.'

Her eyes filled with tears. She was astonished that he immediately grasped something that the people she had spent most time with recently hadn't considered about her current emotional state.

'You must speak to him at his grave, every morning. He will hear you. Promise me you will continue telling him everything that is happening in your life.'

She agreed that she would, although she wasn't at all sure what he meant. She tried to disentangle herself and leave, but he held her tightly. He pulled her towards him and planted a kiss on her face. 'Everything will be alright in the end, don't worry. But tell your children they are not bigger than God – they must remember that.'

On the drive home she told her children what he had said. She wondered aloud if her friend was suffering from some form of madness. Her oldest son was silent for a while before saying, 'But does anyone really know what madness is? We're all composed of different elements – that's all we are in fact – a bunch of compounds nicely packaged in skin. Sometimes one element is in short supply in the brain, and that makes us behave in a way society perceives as abnormal. Who's to say that a madman cannot know and speak the truth?'

'I suppose…'

'While I was sitting with him, every now and then he would excuse himself and turn away from me and speak animatedly to his right. He said he was having a conversation with his brother. There was no one there – but I swear I felt someone's presence. He told me he still speaks to the people he loved once and who are now dead.'

They fell silent in their own remembering. When they arrived home they sat on the veranda, drank tea, smoked cigarettes and spoke into the night of other things.

*

A few days later she saw her friend again. This time she was alone. He was much calmer than he had been that first evening. They sat together at one of the many small cafés that had sprung up in carefully manicured gardens in the northern suburbs. The sun shone through the leaves of the trees making a dappled pattern on their table. They spent the afternoon together. She smoked while he reminisced about the life they had both lived in the old Zimbabwe when they were much younger. They discussed whether remembered memories are true only because we want them to be.

Out of the blue he asked her if she wanted to drive to Mozambique with him.

'Do you have a car?' she asked puzzled.

'Don't act like a crazy person – you know I don't have a car. But I need someone with a car and I need to get to the sea. You have a car, or your son does, anyway.'

'Why – what's at the sea?'

'The sea, of course. So you like to act like a mad person or maybe you're not acting.

She smiled and lit another cigarette. 'Well I… maybe. I'm not sure. I don't have anything else I need to do, I suppose. I have to think about it. I haven't been there in years. But I always say I would like to visit Vilanculos again.'

'It's nothing romantic between us. We are just friends – old good friends, remember. I have no interest in that!' he said pointing down at his trousers.

She laughed a little nervously and drew deeply on her cigarette.

'I have money for fuel,' he said, pulling out a large wad of hundred dollar bills. 'I can pay for everything if you bring your driving licence and, of course, something to drive.'

Later, she would not remember actually agreeing to go, speaking the words outside her head. But it was as if something had passed between the two of them; he knew she would agree to go if he mentioned his longing and she knew she would go as soon as he issued the invitation. She spoke to her son. It would be just for a few days and she needed a reliable car. He shrugged.

Eventually he conceded she could take his 4x4 but he hoped she realised that her friend was unstable at times, at many times in fact. There were stories, plenty of stories. But she didn't feel it would serve any useful purpose to hear them because she was already committed to going, and more than that, she wanted to go.

*

They didn't bother with planning or visas and left at dawn a few days later. She collected him from a shabby block of flats in Belvedere. Before he climbed into the vehicle he turned and looked back at the block for a few minutes without speaking. She would remember that look later.

They stopped overnight in the Vumba where she had a friend, Fiona, who greeted them happily and, as they sat and drank tea, she confessed almost immediately to her two friends that she was quite lonely.

'All of us are lonely,' he said later. 'The idea that human beings are sociable animals is a myth. We are as the animals out there.' He swept a long arm towards the bush as they sat on the veranda overlooking Mozambique. 'Predators and prey all bunched together. Death is the great leveller as we all die in the end.'

There was an awkward silence and then he laughed. No one could laugh the way he did, a deep rumble that started in his diaphragm and passed by his heart before it erupted from his mouth. If that sound could be captured it could surely be used to cure all human ills. The two women laughed with him, and then they continued speaking of more mundane matters.

Their lack of preparation for the long journey turned out to be of little consequence. Machipanda border post was almost deserted as traffic between Mozambique and Zimbabwe had virtually stopped after Renamo activity along the road linking Beira and Maputo increased.

The time they spent travelling in the vehicle was good time. He spoke to her in a gentle voice about life, love and loss. He had brought very little luggage but he had an eclectic selection of CDs. They played at full blast, at his request, as they drove along. Sometimes when they stopped for fuel, or to allow her to stretch her legs and have coffee from the flask Fiona had given her, they would just stand silently together.

'We could have been soulmates in another life,' she said once solemnly.

'No, we are soulmates in this life,' he corrected her. 'Most people, including you it seems, don't know what a soulmate really is. A soulmate comes into someone's life to stir the soul. Once the mission is over they go their separate ways. That's what will happen with us. You see this journey... as soon as I saw you again after all those years I knew we would go on this journey together. I think my ancestors brought you back to Zimbabwe. Agh – I know you are maiguru, but you have stayed on. Why? You must surely have another life in that other place where you live now.'

He never appeared to have much need to hear her responses to the things he said. Most of his conversations were with himself. He always chided her when she asked innocently if he was speaking to her. He spoke to the dead people he had loved so much in life, he said with an impatient sigh. They were his constant companions.

'I have seen this journey in my dreams. So maybe I was not as mad as everyone suspected. I was simply restless because I hadn't made this journey.'

There were times when he would abruptly fall silent and she knew to play another CD. She glanced at him when he slept as she drove. He would turn slightly in his seat and rest his head on the headrest. A small smile would play on his lips, and he would whisper, but so quietly she couldn't hear what he was saying against the noise of the wind and the music. He insisted both front windows had to be open as they drove.

It took almost the entire day to get to Vilanculos. When they arrived they drove along the sandy road that hugged the coast. They parked and walked down to the water's edge as the sun set in the west. He said there was no need for them to book into a hotel or a hostel. They would eat and sit on the beach until they slept, lulled by the sounds of the waves as the sea was the mother of all living things, the great comforter. She shook her head. 'I've been driving all day. I need to stand under a hot shower and sleep under a mosquito net! My friend Donna Margie once lived nearby, perhaps she is still there and will allow us to stay.'

They drove further along the road until she recognised the house that stood on a small mound overlooking the sea. Fortunately, they found Donna Margie at home. She had no other guests and said they could stay a few nights until her next booking.

'Who is this guy?' she asked when the two women were alone. 'He's a bit weird. You do know that.'

'He is a soulmate, a friend, not a lover. But he can look deep into my soul and see…'

'It sounds like you're a bit weird too. Why did you…?'

There were too many questions to know where to start answering them, and equally too many answers. 'He came into this café one evening. People say he is mad. He has episodes, but when we are together what he says… well it makes perfect sense to me. Does that mean that I am crazy too?' As she said that she realised her voice had stopped but her thoughts continued inside her head. Maybe she was mad, for she found she could not rise above the grief she had known these past months.

She stood under a hot shower in the tiny bathroom while he walked down to the sea alone. She dressed. She went and stood by the hedge, smoking, watching him. At first, she could make out only his shadow vaguely outlined in the darkness. As the huge yellow moon rose above the water she could see him more clearly. The evening grew silent and still. Above them, the sky hung heavy with the stars seen only where there is little electric light.

He sat cross-legged on the beach so that when the little waves broke they rushed towards him and lapped over his folded legs. Further down the shore, brightly coloured wooden dhows were anchored, swaying with the movement of the water, waiting for the fishermen to come from their village and for the tide to carry them to the good fishing grounds. She thought she could hear his muted voice, maybe muttering his mantra, 'we are all deeply flawed human beings'. Sometimes he would raise his arms as if calling to someone in the sea. She watched, then lit another cigarette and sat on the wooden bench waiting, but still he sat enveloped in his own world. Eventually she called to him, asking if he wanted to come with her and find somewhere to eat.

'I am not hungry. You can go and eat but I will stay, sit here on the sand.'

The following morning he was sitting on the bench in the garden when she woke up. The two old friends sat mostly in a comforting silence. They ate papaya and granadillas fresh from the market and drank herb tea. A gentle breeze blew in from the ocean tinkling the wind chimes that hung from the thatched roof. The day passed happily. For much of it they sat under the coconut palm and he sketched, or sang the songs that had once made him famous. She read her book. When he sang she stopped reading, closed her eyes, and listened. As the day got hot, they strolled down to the beach and swam in the sea, she in a costume and he still in his trousers. They spoke of the people they had in common. Later, as dusk approached, he came over to her and held her face, 'This has been the perfect day for me. Thank you and thank me.'

*

That evening the three of them walked to the nearby restaurant. His damp khaki trousers flapped against his legs. He said there was no need to change, as they would dry soon enough, besides, he added casually, he hadn't brought any other clothes with him. They ate overlooking the sea, sitting on the slightly uneven surface of a grassy bank. He took ages making sure the table didn't wobble, 'I just can't eat at a wobbly table.' He knelt down folding cardboard strips he had torn from the menu.

She could tell Donna Margie was enjoying their company – especially his. He barely touched his food, but drank several Manicas. He spoke in his usual riddles that had the ring of wisdom in a world where so little made sense. When they had finished eating, he offered to recite some poetry and the two women readily accepted. He rose dramatically to his feet and drew in a deep breath before he began with his loud booming voice. He was a tall handsome man whose greying hair and beard merely added to his stature. They were not his poems but ones he loved, which he recited from memory. The other diners applauded when he eventually sat down. A couple of the other customers came over to thank him personally. He smiled demurely. Then it was time to go.

As they walked back – this time along the beach, he hung back, getting further and further behind the two women. When they reached the gate that led up to the small house, he called to his friend, 'Come and sit with me. I am not ready to sleep yet.'

Donna Margie continued in, leaving the two of them together.

'It was a much wiser man than me who said we should not resist the changes that come our way in life. We must go with the flow. Do you agree?'

Before she could answer, he sat down and gestured her to sit next to him. 'Sometimes when there is great pain, tears will wash that pain away. I have seen your tears and the way you still cry for him. But sometimes tears are not enough... too weak. And then...' he waved his arm towards the sea.

'And then what?'

'It's hard to believe you had such a privileged education. There is so much that you do not seem to know.' There was a hint of impatience in his voice, but it vanished after he paused for a moment. 'Salt water – it's the cure for everything. Sometimes that cure can come from the sweat of hard work, sometimes it comes from the tears we weep, but sometimes when the pain is too deep, only the sea can heal.'

He continued while gazing out toward the horizon almost invisible in the inky night, 'In some cultures they refer to death as crossing the river. Do you suppose when there is no river and just the sea you can cross the sea?'

'Maybe.' Her voice was soft.

'You know, driving me here, no one has ever done such a selfless thing for me on such a whim. I know you were worried and, frankly, even I was surprised both you and your son agreed. He has seen me on a bad day.'

She smiled, but did not speak.

'It was Tagore who said 'You smiled and talked to me of nothing and I felt that for this I had been waiting long' and there you are smiling at me and talking of nothing.'

She leaned against him, feeling part of her loneliness ebb away.

*

She felt herself dozing off every now and then, but he continued speaking as if his body was simply emptying out all the words it had once held. He spoke of his childhood and the terrible losses he had suffered during the liberation war and afterwards. Most of the time his pain was more than one soul could possibly bear. Above them the meteorite shower went unnoticed. He spoke through the night and into the first light of the new day. He spoke of all the things that dwelt inside him. He knew the Nirvana where all previous lives fell away.

Suddenly he shook her, 'Come on sleepyhead.' He got to his feet and pulled her up. 'It's time for the healing.'

He took off his shirt and folded it neatly before tossing it down onto the sand. She took off her skirt but kept her t-shirt on for the sake of modesty. Then he stretched out his hand towards her, 'Come.'

They stepped into the sea through the gentle waves. The water of the Indian Ocean has a peculiar warmth. In spite of that she gasped as it rose past her waist. He turned to her before he let go her hand, 'Whatever I tell you to do in the sea, you must do it. Promise me that now.'

She thought he was joking but his face was serious.

'Promise me that now.'

She nodded.

He continued, 'I can't remember any time I felt as happy and as lucid as I do at this moment. Please remember that.'

He let go of her hand and dived into a swell. She followed suit and together they swam slowly further and further out to sea. He stopped swimming and floated on his back for a while. He was panting gently with the effort of the swimming. They could not touch the sea floor for the water was too deep. He called her name and she looked at him. 'It's time for you to swim back now.'

'What do you mean?'

'Remember your promise. Go back now. Your children are waiting for you. Your grief will wash away. Your lamp is still burning. It's time for mine to dim now.

'Please…'

'I know I have asked much of you – but this is the last thing I ask. Go back.' He started swimming away from her, strong strokes, as if he was being pulled by an invisible rope.

She floated there for a while watching him before she swam back to the shore. When she got to the beach she looked out towards the horizon, where a red sun was rising. She thought she saw a small dark head bobbing away from her. A fisherman came towards her. He spoke halting English, asking her if she was alright.

'My friend,' she pointed.

He looked in the direction she was pointing. 'There is no one there, madam.'

'My friend.' She started sobbing then and fell to her knees. 'My friend.'

*

Donna Margie translated all she said had happened into Portuguese for the police. They shook their heads. His body was never found. She collected his shirt and the holdall that held the CDs but mainly pieces of paper that had been filled with tiny handwriting. On one he had written 'You can't cross the sea merely by standing and staring at the water'. He had written it over and over again. She found a piece of paper that had been folded, with her name on the outside and a message in his handwriting, 'My cup runneth over, for my time for talking is done. Thank me for the cure.'

She imagined him laughing and she wept.

The Travellers

Tariro Ndoro

If Reuben doesn't stop playing 'Fast Car' on the overhead, I might just jump over the counter and walk right out of this place. We all want to leave without Reuben reminding us that we work a dead end job in a dead end town. Five times I've packed my bags and told myself that, sometime in the middle of my shift, I'll go to the backroom, peel off my franchise uniform and jump onto the next Greyhound to Beitbridge.

I used to dream of finding a lonely gonyet driver to take me to Joburg where the real money is, but my cousin sent me pictures of all the injured Zimbos on Whatsapp after the xenophobic attacks and I've decided that I'd rather be alive here than dead there.

Circles of wind draw spirals carrying red dust – each little grain of dust gets picked up, swirled and dumped again on the sandy stretch of the car park. I am waiting for the next bus. I watch all the buses pass up and down from behind the formica counter of Chicken Inn, Chegutu.

Good afternoon, my name is Gertrude, can I take your order? I've been here since forever, circling job adverts in the *The Sunday Mail* classifieds even though it's Tuesday because I can't afford the paper anymore and I have to wait for Gladys to give me hers.

Reuben doesn't like it when we read the paper on the job, told me once that if I hated my job so much I should just quit because there are a hundred other unemployed girls who would thank God for it, but he knows it's slow before the buses get here and everyone already talks about him for being a douche so he turns a blind eye.

I hate Reuben. He tried to grope me the other day and when I slapped him off he said he'd tell HR so I keep my distance when I can. Besides, I need my job. Didn't really need it when I started here after

93

high school, whiling away the time until the MSU semester began, but then Baba got retrenched from David Whitehead Textiles where he'd commuted every day for the past fifteen years. So here I am three years later, sometimes glad I didn't waste my time with university because Gladys, who works the day shift with me, has a whole degree from Fort Hare but we get the same pay.

We live in a hick town and I want to leave. Chegutu starts at Chicken Inn and ends with Taurai's Motor Parts down the highway and unless you have a farm somewhere there's nothing to do except make plans to leave. We like to stare at the travellers in the buses and make up lives for them. They come in from Harare on their way to Bulawayo or South Africa or Botswana, at least somewhere exciting that isn't here, and they go back the way they came, only stopping here to get a 2 Piecer or use the bathroom. One of them has just come in on the 9 o'clock Tenda, looking sharp in his suit like he is going for a job interview. Gladys asks me what I think of him.

It's a good thing she went to Fort Hare for three years because if she hadn't she would have heard the rumours about Edward. Not that Edward was the man in the suit but he looked a lot like him and if Gladys had been looking at me instead of packing soft drinks into the fridge she would have seen me freeze in space. Edward.

Edward had blown in from Kwekwe during the gold rush, said he owned a mine somewhere there and his sister lived here. Dressed in suits all the time so I should have known that he'd never been near a mine shaft in his whole life. He was just as tall as the smart stranger who is walking towards me now. He promised me the world and everything in it, told me my smile stopped the world for five seconds then made it spin in the opposite direction. Unotenderedza musoro wangu – those had been his words.

Mr Pants Suit is chewing a Dandy Gum, the one that smells like spearmint. He hands me a twenty dollar note and tells me he wants a 2 Piecer and two cans of Coke. Then, in a low voice, he tells me to keep the change and he winks at me. Smooth.

Too bad I know his kind. The ones that walk in here every day, on the 2 pm Greyhound, the 11 am Pathfinder, the 5.15 pm City to City; all of them wear dress shirts and jackets with their jeans, top it off with the kind of shoes pastors like to wear these days, mess around on their phones and talk really loudly in English so we can all hear their good accents and be amazed by their million dollar business deals. Nyoka.

Mr Pants Suit's order is ready and when he takes it he leaves his number on the counter but doesn't look at me. I throw the number in the bin and wish there wasn't sweat just beneath my hairnet, then I could look at him as if he's nothing, like Gladys does when the older men come in and ask for our numbers.

Gladys has all sorts of names for stuff like that, like 'rape culture' and 'harassment', but I just know that I feel cheap and dirty when the men off the bus try to fondle my hand when I give them change or when they lean over the counter and talk in low voices like we share some kind of secret when we don't.

Gladys keeps telling me things will get better but I know she's crazy. She was one of those people who said that bond notes wouldn't come and yet here they are and she also said that the drought was made up but she's suffering like the rest of us, coughing her lungs up in the afternoon when the hot wind pushes the red dust around so that we can feel the heat in our dry nostrils.

She isn't tired like the rest of us, she still has dreams that she'll get a proper job at an accounting firm for which she studied. Real dreams, not daydreams, either. Just last night she dreamed of herself in a big office with a great big oak table and people calling her ma'am and everything. She's getting close now, she can feel it, she says. She's been feeling it for six months but I don't tell her that because I know that, if I do, she'll remind me that Joel Osteen says we must only say positive things because that's what makes the good happen.

Gladys just refuses to believe in facts. Like when it didn't rain last year and she said it wouldn't be a drought and now the trees everywhere have wilted and my cousin, who works in Matabeleland, says all the cattle are falling like flies, but Gladys shakes her head and says we should never think the worst. Gladys, who got a full scholarship to go to South Africa and get her degree. What can she tell me about life?

Still, I prefer her to everyone else I've worked with. Last year it was Tsitsi, who was clueless, always got the change wrong or made the customers angry. She was fired after three weeks. Only stayed so long because she's Rueben's uncle's sister's cousin. You know the story.

Before Gladys and Tsitsi there was Portia. Loud, imposing Portia. Acted like she knew everything and maybe I let her act that way; she had two kids already and I was just out of high school. Knew how to keep her husband in line and knew how to handle Rueben too. Introduced me to Edward.

The first time Eddy came to order his quarter chicken and chips, he was really looking for Portia. Had known her from somewhere or other. I wasn't paying attention. All *I* saw was the way he stopped and stared when he saw me. He was the first person to do that. I mean the first proper person to do that, not those dudes that chill by the corner smoking zvimonera and whistling at everything in a skirt.

He came to order his quarter chicken and chips every day after that, became our second regular after Mhofu, the manager at Food & City whose wife left him for an accountant. After a week, he'd bring me something every day and hang around the counter before the rush of buses arrived.

Did I know Eddy was trouble, that it was strange that a man like him liked a girl like me? Maybe. But maybe I also did it to be closer to Portia, who knew how to tell people what's what and who was the first big sister I had since Mama died in '08. Mainini Tambu, my musara pavana, only stayed long enough to pick up Mama's clothes and take her microwave, so Portia's friendship was important to me.

We spent all those hours planning the great escape. Once Edward's mine started making profit we would get married at the Fairmile in Gweru. Portia would be my maid of honour. That was before Edward's face was all over the newspapers for cattle theft. He'd only come here to hide out but a peacock like him can't hide, the same way a lion can't stop eating meat.

What did Portia say when it happened? She'd known it the whole time. That's how he'd been when they were growing up and he lived in the house next door, he charmed people out of money and left countless stupid girls pregnant. Could I tell Portia what I was carrying after she said that? No, I just took care of it like a big girl then went home and packed away all my childhood pictures because I couldn't look at the carefree me anymore, she looked like she was judging me.

A Translux rolls in and another man in fancy clothes hops off, sliding his thumb across his tablet. The sun is scorching but he has his shades on top of his head and he walks purposefully towards me.

Maybe he's another conman travelling to a hideout or maybe he's legit. I'll never know because I will throw his number in the bin when he hands it to me and keep circling jobs in the classifieds.

The Big Noise

Christopher Kudyahakudadirwe

We heard the big noise with our little ears. It was a strange noise. We had never heard a noise that loud except in summer when clouds rose up into the sky, and in them and under them jagged bolts of lightning preceded the empty drum-like rumbling that sent me hiding between Mother's bags of groundnuts behind the door in her kitchen hut. Everyone in my family knew that thunder and lightning were my worst enemies. If a thunderstorm developed and they were about to eat deliciously prepared chicken, I wasn't going to be part of that. And now, coming from some unknown place, the big noise shook the ground and echoed from the hills on the other side of our beautiful valley. The chickens scurried to hide under the granary while the birds flew from the trees and landed on the rooftops of our huts – something that they had never done before, considering the fact that we trapped them, shot them and stole their young as well as their eggs. Normally they kept their distance so as not to be hit by the stones we threw. But this time the confused birds tweeted loudly and almost flew into the huts where we kept the pots in which we would cook them.

The village was often quiet in the hot summer afternoon, but on this day, the mighty sound disturbed the peace and increased in volume as if it was drawing closer. We felt it inside our bodies; it rattled our chests and rocked our feet. We searched this way and that way; upwards and downwards but nothing appeared on the horizon. We looked silent and fearful questions at each other. It was just too complicated for two little boys like us to understand. We wished our parents were there to explain to us what was happening. All this time our hearts thumped like mortars being worked by over-aged girls who had lost glorious opportunities to get married.

We looked around for suitable hiding places, perhaps under the granary where the chickens had taken refuge? But what if the thing that was making the huge noise was much larger than our granary? Wouldn't we be flattened under it? I imagined dying under the granary together with our chickens and perhaps all the rats in the homestead. We looked at the big mukuyu tree that stood in the middle of the homestead. Would we be safe up there from where the birds had flown? Maybe the birds, because they were always up above us, had seen the thing whose noise had drowned every other sound in the village. And if so, the thing would not find it difficult to pluck us from that tree just like ripe figs ready for the mouth. We looked at the lush bush that surrounded our home, but those were only bushes; they were not thick enough to make us invisible. Moreover, if the thing were tall, then it was not a good idea to seek a hiding place there. We looked at the river – our big river. It ran just a spitting distance from the village. Our minds discarded that idea because a week before one of our calves had been dragged into the water by a crocodile. Father only found its head stashed in the caves on the opposite bank the following day. Our grandfather, the father of my father, had recently told us to keep our shadows away from the waters of this mighty river lest a crocodile drag us in by our shadows. And which one of us would like to die between the yellow teeth of that monster?

The most unfortunate thing was that we were all alone at home. Our parents and older siblings had gone to the fields for the second shift of the day's weeding. We had been left 'looking after' the home. The two of us were supposed to play guard, but the booming sound that was creeping upon us had reduced us to cowards rather than the warriors of valour that we were meant to be. The noise grew louder by the minute. When I looked at my brother, who was a year older than me, I saw fear stamped all over his face. But what really shocked me was the river of yellowish liquid that streamed down his shins to his bare feet. His bladder must have given in and surrendered to the fear-inducing sound that we had never heard in our valley.

'Let's follow the elders to the fields,' I suggested in between the chattering of my teeth.

'Nonsense! That's where the thing making the noise is coming from. You don't want to walk yourself into its mouth.' My brother quickly nullified my 'good' idea.

'You're right.' I felt my foolishness mix with the fear of the approaching unknown demon. 'That thing must be huge and the mouth that gives out such a huge noise must be huge too. We will be eaten alive.'

We wondered why our parents had not run back home from the fields. Had the approaching monster eaten them already? If our parents had been eaten who were we to survive the threat of death that had taken our parents and older siblings? These questions made me feel helpless and it was then I felt the hot yellow liquid coursing down my grey shins too. My brother looked at me but saw nothing funny in this.

Then, as we pondered what to do, where to hide and when to do what we had to do, we both looked where the horrendous noise was coming from, and there, just above the tree tops we saw plumes of black smoke shooting into the afternoon air. Our imaginations ran wild.

'Could it be a big fire coming to roast us alive?' I asked my brother.

'I don't want to know.' Like me he was shivering as if he had just finished having a forced cold bath in winter.

Sekuru, our mother's brother, the one who came home at the end of the year with packets of sweet things and bread and jam and clothes for us, once told us about a place high above the clouds where bad people were roasted on a fire that did not die down.

'Do you remember?' I asked my brother.

'I don't want to remember, please!' My brother was almost crying.

We scarpered behind the granary just to avoid seeing the approaching black smoke and whatever was making it. A giant rat suddenly came scrambling from the eaves of the roof to fall right at our feet. We screamed as we jumped backwards simultaneously. The rat scampered under the granary and we ran back where we had come from.

Meanwhile the huge noise, by now, was almost upon us but still, because of the thick bush, we could not see what was causing it. The smoke was now drifting towards us. It smelt like Father's sandals when an ember of burning wood fell on one of them. Judging from the different pitches of the deep-throated growls we were now quite sure that it was not one thing but several of them approaching our home. We scurried around like confused ants whose nest has been unintentionally trampled by a cow. The home, our home, had become a place of insecurity.

Then the first one appeared.

It was bigger than the elephants that visited our maize racks at night to rob us of our year's pumpkin and maize harvest. It was nhundurwa in colour and had large hand-like extensions that looked like the back legs of a grasshopper. These supported a huge knife-like scoop that looked like it had cut through a lot of things in its life. Under it we could see chain-like things which plodded ahead like the feet of a very large elephant, one at a time like a fast-moving snail. Above it was a big black pipe that belched out the black plumes of smoke that we had seen above the treeline. The monster crushed trees that were in its path like grass after a heavy storm. It was such a mesmerising creature that we froze on the spot for a short while. Though filled with fear, I admired the power and the unstoppable desire of the thing to destroy anything in its path.

We did not wait to see the others stop just outside our home. We dashed to the back of our mother's kitchen hut where the granary stood. I slid under and pushed to one side where the chickens that had also taken refuge were. My chest was almost bursting with fear and my mouth was dry. I could feel the warm liquid wetting my 10 oz shorts again where I lay with my face buried in the dusty ground under the granary. The loud noises had now subsided to a quiet drone similar to that produced by the black wasps that often built their nests in the conical roof of Mother's cooking hut. Then we heard voices. Some of them I could not identify but I heard Father's voice distinctly. It was not his usual one. It seemed he was not happy. Some of what the other people were saying did not make sense to us. I looked in the direction from where the voices came. I saw Father's feet – I couldn't mistake those tyre sandals that he had been wearing since time immemorial – and another pair in black boots that shone like the outside of Mother's clay cooking pots.

'The bwana says a big dam is going to be built here whether you like it or not,' someone who spoke our language said.

'Ask your bwana whether we were ever informed of that. How can government do that to us? Are we not citizens of this country?' Father asked. His feet shifted the way they always did when he was angry. I could clearly imagine his facial expression as he asked these questions. From under the granary I could not tell how the people he was talking to looked. I watched more pairs of feet lifting up and down as their owners walked about our yard.

Then I saw Mother's cracked feet walking all over the place. They went to the mukuyu tree and then came back to the cooking hut. Sometimes they stopped. The feet went to my parents' sleeping hut and remained there for quite a while. Why was she moving around like that? Could she be looking for us? I, for one, was not going to come out and be devoured by those big monsters that were now droning and puffing at the edge of our home like tired hunting dogs after a long day of chasing rabbits.

'Chamunorwa! Munorwei!' I heard the thin voice of Mother call our names. I looked at Munorwei. He looked back at me. I now thought: if we come out of hiding, would those monsters eat us in the presence of our mother and father? Mother would not allow that. She loved us, her children, very much. She would fight for us as she did when our big sister had a problem with the boy from the home next door. I was much younger then, but I remember how Mother bit the mother of that boy with her big white teeth that turned red with the other woman's blood. The details of what had happened to provoke that fight are not clear to me even today.

'Chamu! Muno!' Mother called again. 'Now, where are those children?' she asked no one in particular.

As we watched, her feet came towards the granary. She opened the door and climbed inside. We heard her rummaging through the sacks of maize and mhunga that she kept there. Her feet could be heard thudding above us. Then they climbed down and we saw her knees and hands touching the ground. And finally, her face looked at us. We crawled out with our wet shorts covered in dust.

By mid-May we had finished gathering our crops from the fields. The date for our relocation was almost upon us. Our goats and donkeys were now free ranging in the fields, eating the remnants of the maize crop. We went about hunting mice and grasshoppers to supplement our food. The huge machines that had come two months earlier had already started work at the place where the mountains constricted the river valley. Every day we heard them groaning and bellowing there. We did not know what they were really doing, as we were never allowed to wander far from home. We heard that they had come to build a huge dam. As children, we were never told what that meant. The snippets of information that came our way were gleaned from the adults, who always spoke in hushed tones about not wanting to be relocated far away from the land of their ancestors and from the graves of their forefathers. We did not understand some of these things; they were too complicated for our simple little minds. We heard that the dam was going to be very useful to many people in that it would provide lots of water and fish. We did not see any sense in that because our river gave enough water for our winter crops and there were fish as big as myself that people caught. The adults also said that the dam was going to be used for generating electricity, which would benefit the country. Which country and what was that animal called electricity? We asked ourselves these questions when we were out chasing birds and grasshoppers in the valley. We did not know that there was something called a country at all. Our horizon and the hills that stood at the edge of the valley defined our life and our existence under the sun.

For more than a week, the men of the village gathered at my father's dare to exchange views in hushed voices about something that we could not understand. The only words that we heard and heard clearly were that we, the children, should never be allowed to hear what they were talking about because we had small hearts. Even our mothers were kept away from these discussions. But in the secrecy of their daily deliberations we heard words like nyakanyaka, vana vevhu and vapambepfumi. And when the men of the village said these words they were very angry and punched the air with their clenched fists, but we did not see anyone with whom they were angry. Sometimes they ended the meeting by singing a song that we had never heard before. One late afternoon we sang the song while going to fetch the goats from the river and Father took a green stick and thrashed our dusty legs telling us never to sing that song again.

One night, I woke up suddenly. I thought I was dreaming, but I was not. In the darkness, I clearly heard someone calling Father's name. After three calls his sleeping hut door made its usual sound when someone opened it from inside. Then I heard his tyre-sandal clad feet crunching the gravel as he walked away from home. I wondered where he was going and who was calling him at that time of the night. I had heard that witches can call people if they want to ride them like horses to go and attend to their business. I tried to wake my brother but he was not one who was easily disturbed at night when he was sleeping. His snoring increased when I shook him and became even deeper, so I gave up and left him like that.

When the last drongo chirped on the mukuyu tree indicating that day was about to break, I heard the crunching gravel again. This time I got up on my elbows and peeped through the gap between the doorframe and the door to see Father walking towards the granary. He looked tired. On his shoulder was a shovel. This was strange to me. I tried to make sense of it but my mind fell short of solving the mystery of the shovel and the night disappearance. He threw the shovel under the granary before going into his sleeping hut. He did not come out until midday when Mother went to give him food.

Two days, three days, four days went by quietly without incident. On the fifth day, early in the morning, we were roused by loud banging on my parents' door. Night had not yet said goodbye to the valley but the east was ripening into day slowly. I looked through the crack to see two men standing at my parents' door. Father came out half-dressed. The two men immediately grabbed him and put his arms behind him. Why his arms remained there I could not understand because I knew Father as a very strong man who could carry heavy logs from the forest when Mother wanted to make beer. One of the men hit Father on the head with what looked like a thick stick and he swayed like a tree that was about to fall after being cut but he didn't hit the ground because the other man kicked him in the stomach and he came up straight. Mother came out screaming at the top of her voice. I scrambled out of my blankets and ran to the scene. That's when I heard screams from other homes in the village.

'How can you burn equipment belonging to the government?' one of the men said, pushing Mother to the ground. 'We will teach you a lesson you will never forget before we throw you in jail. The dam project you want to stop has cost government a lot of money and you think you are more important than the project. We will show you that government is more powerful than you.' Baton blows rained on Father as the man spoke. Who was this person called government who wanted to build a dam in our village? Why didn't that person build it somewhere else? These questions and many others troubled my small mind.

By now the sun was coming up over the eastern horizon. The men drove Father, kicking him and whacking him with the black batons, to where their leader, a white man, was waiting. More village men were herded there, all with their hands tied at the back. From where I stood with Mother I could see that these men, like Father, had been thoroughly beaten. Some had blood on their shirtfronts while others, men I knew not to have limps before, were limping like their legs had been broken. I did not understand why these strong men from my village, men who would kill an elephant or a lion with spears, did not fight back.

Before long, most of the men of our village had been forced to sit down in front of the white man. They looked defeated and dejected. From a distance, we heard the drone of a lorry climbing down the valley using the same way that was used by the big machines that our fathers were said to have burned, forcing their drivers to run away. It arrived in a flurry of dust and smoke. The men were loaded into it before being driven away to a place we did not know.

The following week a convoy of very green lorries arrived in the valley. Our mothers and brothers loaded some of our belongings into them. We were not allowed to take our goats with us because the lorries were full. We sat on top of our belongings and the lorries drove out of the valley slowly, swaying like drunken giants on the uneven road, as if giving us time to say goodbye to our ancestors' graves. As we topped the hills, we saw plumes of smoke going up to join the afternoon clouds.

'My children,' Mother said, wiping tears from her eyes, 'don't look back, because you will never come back here again.'

Sand City

Ignatius Mabasa

The rain clouds came quietly, like a smooth criminal. Like startled birds flying from a tree, the rain was sudden and noisy. It chased away all the children who were playing next to the road. Some had been pushing broken bricks in the sand – playing maverick kombi drivers and police officers at roadblocks. Others had been building houses and roads with the sand, a sand city.

Screaming with excitement, and because of the coldness of water droplets on their skins, the children abandoned their fun and games. Joe rushed towards his home, but suddenly stopped. He turned to look at the beautiful sand city he had poured his heart into, and felt each water drop that struck it also peck mercilessly at his heart like a hungry crow.

He wished he could have carried the sand city into the house, but knew that no dirt was allowed indoors. Also the city was not personal property. It belonged to the group – police, kombi drivers and construction workers.

A big drop of rain splashed on his left temple and rolled down to his jaw. He brushed the tickling water with his hand, and darted into the house.

'And leave your dirty shoes there by the door,' his mother ordered.

Joe bent to untie and remove his tatty, smelly tennis shoes. He was grumbling inaudibly, 'Mother thinks everything about me is dirty. Dirty clothes, dirty shoes, dirty hair, dirty hands, dirty legs.'

He left the shoes behind the kitchen door and went into one of the bedrooms that faced the road where he had been playing. He approached the window and parted the heavy curtains. Outside, the rain was now falling fast. He watched small rivulets form around the sand city. They filled the small gulleys and depressions before eroding the sand city, the roads and roadblocks. Joe felt like shouting to the foamy brownish waters not to wash their city away. The raindrops shelled and pummelled the earth, and soon everything outside became fuzzy and blurred.

The noise of falling rain was deafening. Joe stood stock still behind the curtains, looking at the rain. Not a thing was now visible outside. Joe sighed hard against the windowpane, and the condensation spread like a ghost's wedding gown. He started drawing and doodling on the window. After what seemed like an age, he noticed the rain was thinning. He could see puddles here and there.

And, as if it had not been raining at all, a beaming sun came out. It transformed everything outside.

One, two, three... Joe saw his friends run out of their houses, jump and splash in the puddles. Joe's eyes bulged in excitement as he thought of rebuilding the sand city. He untangled himself from behind the curtains and ran out to join his friends. Playing in the mud was fun for the boys. They threw stones into the dirty water, kicked, ran and screamed.

One of them, Tawana, moved towards the hedge looking for stones to throw. Then he saw IT, A yellow-green bullfrog with big black eyes.

'Joe... Kuda... Kodza... come, come and see!' Tawana shouted with a trembling, excited voice.

The other boys ran to Tawana. Their mouths dropped open in surprise.

'That is a monster frog!' Kodza shouted.

'I think it is coming from hell,' said Joe, breathing fast.

Kuda picked up a long stick and poked the frog in its pot-belly. It quickly jumped twice, and the boys scattered sniggering. As fast as they had dispersed, they gathered again around the frog.

'Look at the throat. It's dancing,' said Kodza.

'Let's KILL IT,' Joe suggested.

'What for?' Kuda asked.

'I hate frogs, that's why,' said a newly arrived girl called Thenjiwe.

'But if you kill the frog, Satan will burn you,' said Kuda.

'Let's kill it just a little then,' Tawana reasoned.

'But if you kill it a little, it will still die,' Kuda said, getting worried.

'If it dies we will bury it and put a cross on its grave so that it can go to heaven,' suggested Joe.

'But that doesn't help because such ugly frogs don't go to heaven,' Thenjiwe explained.

Kuda was not comfortable with killing the frog, 'Thenjiwe, you are a girl, and you are supposed to be kind and merciful.'

'How do you know, maybe I am a boy.' Thenjiwe laughed while guarding the frog from escaping into the nearby hedge.

Noticing the determination of his friends, Kuda gave up, 'You can go ahead and kill it, but the frog has not done anything to anyone. Don't say I didn't warn you, but the frog can come to your house at night asking why you killed it.'

Joe laughed, 'If it comes to our house asking me why I killed it, I will kill it again.'

The other children laughed, but Kuda was upset, 'I will report you to your mothers.'

Tawana replied, 'If you tell our mothers, we will never play with you again.'

Joe added, 'So you now have a new friend, this stupid frog.'

Kuda turned his back and walked away. From his house he could hear the cheers and shouts from his friends. He knew that every cheer and shout meant something terrible being done to the frog.

Outside, Thenjiwe was given a handful of stones to pelt the frog. She missed. Then it was Kodza's turn. Kodza hit the frog on the head. There were loud cheers. The frog looked stunned. Then it started bleeding through the eyes, mouth and nose.

Joe was next. All his pebbles missed and he got angry. He fetched a big stone and squashed the poor frog with it. The stone rolled over leaving behind a bloody frog with intestines hanging out and legs twitching.

As the children were studying the effects of Joe's bomb, he was called by his sister, Saru, to go and bathe.

Joe did not like being washed. He always argued that he was now old enough to bathe on his own, but his mother never agreed, saying that Joe played with dirt until he resembled a pig, and that only a thorough scrubbing made him look human again.

As Saru was drying him, Joe asked, 'Do frogs follow you if you kill them?'

Saru laughed, 'Yes, especially if you kill them for no particular reason.'

Joe was silent.

At supper, he ate very little food. He was thinking about the frog and what Saru had said. His mother threatened to use the stick in order to make him eat, but that did not help.

That evening, Joe developed a fever. The fever degenerated into hallucinating. Joe screamed and held his mother tightly. There was fear written all over his thin face.

Sobbing, he said, 'The frog is knocking at our door. I see it. It has blood coming out of its mouth, nose and ears.' His mother had no idea what the boy was talking about. Joe continued, 'I see it. It is now inside the house. It is looking for me.'

Joe was sick in bed for two days. He had a fever and nightmares. He had no appetite. On the third day, he turned a corner. He woke up and ate some maize porridge. Afterwards, he went to sit outside and bask in the sun. He could see his friends playing kombi drivers and cops. Others were building a city – roads, bridges and speed humps. Joe's heart burned with the desire to join his friends. He stood up and tottered to the play site.

'Hey, Joe is here!' Tawana shouted, sniffing some stubborn mucus back.

All his friends looked at him as he slowly squatted at the edge of the sand city.

'What do you want to be today Joe? Kombi driver or cop?' Kuda asked, looking at his other friends as if to seek approval.

Kodza slowly shook his head, 'Remember we agreed.'

Joe asked, 'Agreed to do what?'

'The burial,' replied Tawana.

'What burial?' Joe asked, looking tired and old.

'The frog must be buried properly or else it will be angry,' Kodza explained.

Joe looked at the spot where he last saw the frog. It was covered with sticks and leaves. Flies were having a rally there, but they also seemed to be having a disagreement about something. Joe sniffed the air as if he wanted to say something, but he didn't.

Kuda said, 'I can provide a coffin. I have a shoebox under my bed.'

'And I can get the shovel for digging,' Kodza offered.

'So what must I do?' Joe asked, sounding confused.

'You will say a prayer for the frog,' Tawana said firmly.

Joe looked as if he wanted to speak and cry at the same time.

Kuda ran to his house and came back with a yellow and red shoebox. He asked Kodza whether he had brought the shovel.

Kodza grinned, 'In a moment, constable.' He quickly disappeared behind the sickly hedge that fronted their house.

When Kodza came back with the shovel, he found the other children surrounding Joe, who was lying on top of the newly built sand city. Whitish slimy stuff came from his mouth and he croaked due to the choking vomit.

Thenjiwe came running and peered at Joe. She jumped back, 'The spirit of the frog has got him. He is going to die.'

Saru heard the commotion from the house and rushed outside to investigate. She found Joe croaking, trying to clear his throat. The boys and Thenjiwe were now standing away from the sand city. Saru lifted Joe up, made him sit and helped him wipe his mouth. She took the shovel from Kodza, and scooped sand from the sand city buildings and roads and bridges to cover the vomit.

Joe pleaded weakly with Saru to use some of the sand to cover the dead frog under the sticks and leaves. The rotting smell of the frog was nauseating him, making him want to vomit again.

Saru dug up more city buildings and completely covered the spot where the dead frog lay. The rallying flies were angry and staged a demo, but Saru used the back of the shovel to ram and level the sand, leaving a beautiful-looking grave for the frog.

She handed the shovel back to Kodza and helped Joe stand up. They trudged into their yard and closed the gate behind them.

Divine Intervention

Barbara Mhangami-Ruwende

Tawanda placed the phone on its cradle. He inhaled deeply and held his breath, trying to calm himself down. Thinking that it might help control his anger, he exhaled very slowly. He had just got off the phone with his mother in Zimbabwe and, as was always the case after a conversation with her, he felt disjointed and furious. Tawanda hated feeling this way. Every couple of weeks after his habitual call home, he vowed never to call again, but, two weeks later, on a Sunday afternoon, he picked up the phone and dialled her number, as if amnesia had wiped out the sour memory of the previous conversation. The cause of his ire was not his mother, or the fact that he felt obliged to call her. No, in fact, he always looked forward to hearing her voice. If only they could have a different conversation. It was always the same topic, Tawanda's elder brother Caleb. Tawanda wished that, if it was imperative to discuss Caleb, then, just for once, the story would be a positive, uplifting tale of transformation or some sort of success, such as finding a job and moving out of his mother's house. But it was always the same tale of woe and disaster, which was never Caleb's fault. On the contrary, Caleb was the perpetual victim of charlatans, crooks, liars, man-eating amazons and circumstance. Tawanda was invariably his saviour, the one who sent home the pounds to pay back the ruthless moneylenders who demanded 100% interest on a loan. He spent an inordinate amount of time at the Western Union wiring money to pay for antibiotics to treat Caleb's carelessly acquired syphilis or a loan to start a small and yet unnamed business. Every time he heard the requests for money to bail out Caleb, he swore that it was the last time.

111

Yet the pitiable sound of his mother's tired, anxiety-drenched voice was enough to have him asking, 'How much is required, Mama?'

He hated himself for being so weak and he resented his mother for manipulating him and using emotional blackmail to force him to send the money.

'Don't worry, Mama. It is no problem. I will text you the money transfer number tomorrow. Just text me when you get the money.'

He feigned lightness and injected false happiness into his voice as he asked after her health. Her response would turn the taste in his mouth bitter, as though he had chewed on the pulp of a grapefruit. 'I am very well, just worried about Caleb who is languishing here. Honestly, Tawanda, you must do something. He is your elder brother and it is not right that you are successful and he is not. Can you not bring him over there so he can work in your company? You know it is better to have family in your business because, even if they steal from you, at least it's family and not strangers reaping where they did not sow.'

Tawanda sighed as he looked out of his council flat at the corner of Byres Road and University Avenue. He had not bothered to move after completing his degree in pharmacology at the University of Glasgow two years before. It was cheap because he had a roommate, Tunde from Lagos. He liked being close to the university campus. He had landed a job with GlaxoSmithKline Pharmaceuticals and could afford to move into a more spacious, upscale abode. However, he reasoned that living near the academic world would keep alive his dream of pursuing doctoral studies. Of course, this would have to be after Caleb was doing alright.

Caleb. Tawanda felt his jaw tightening and his teeth clenching tightly, sending a spasm of pain down the sides of his neck. He tried to ease the tension by stretching the tendons in his neck, tilting his head first to the left, then to the right. He sighed again, feeling a little lighter of heart. Suddenly he had a brilliant idea.

Caleb had developed a wound of unknown origin on his leg. According to his mother, Caleb just woke up with a gaping sore on his left shin and, because of its mysterious appearance, Caleb and she thought it must be of a spiritual origin rather than a medical condition. Several months had gone by and his mother lamented that the lesion had become a pus-oozing mess that smelt foul. Caleb adamantly refused to seek medical help and was instead frequenting the Apostles of Johannes, who bathed him every other day in the murky waters of the Umguza River and prayed and fasted for his healing. Apparently, there had been a prophecy that someone in the family, on Tawanda's side, was responsible for Caleb's general bad luck and the state of his leg. Money was needed (not as payment, NEVER as payment) to bring in a powerful man of God from Malawi, who would undo the curse and deliver Caleb from his physical, spiritual and financial afflictions. Added to this was the prophecy of a nubile 14-year-old virgin as the first of many wives for Caleb.

'Enough of this madness,' Tawanda thought to himself. 'I am getting myself on a plane to Zimbabwe and I will deal with this foolishness once and for all!'

Two weeks later, Tawanda boarded a South African Airways flight from Heathrow Airport. Eleven hours later, he would be in Johannesburg where he would catch a connecting flight to Bulawayo. As he settled in his seat, he felt excitement at the thought of seeing his mother again after five years. He had been meaning to return home for a visit, but somehow the time was never quite right. Well, now was as good a time as any and he looked forward to spending quality time with her and seeing all his relatives. Although he had never given it much thought, Tawanda missed home. He was well settled in Glasgow, and had very good friends and a decent enough social life. Apart from the disgusting sidewalks with sporadic piles of dog shit and splatterings of vomit on Saturday mornings after Friday night binge drinking, Tawanda really liked Glasgow and Glaswegians. He engaged in casual dating but had not yet met anyone he felt passionate enough about to get serious. At twenty-six, he took comfort in knowing that he had plenty of time. Besides, his mother had made it abundantly clear that he could not get married before his elder brother settled down with someone. It would not look right and people would talk.

Caleb was thirty-four years old, handsome and tall. When they were younger, he would charm the local storekeeper into giving him ten sweets when he had only paid for five. He had doe-like brown eyes, a cute pout and a tight, pert backside that landed him his first sexual experience at the age of 14. It had been with their maid, Sisi Thoko, who had been unceremoniously fired shortly thereafter. Poor girl, thought Tawanda. She was only eighteen and Caleb was irresistible.

She had been accused of turning mother's precious son out. Little did Mother know that Caleb had been sneaking out to the servants' quarters for months before the act took place, begging Thoko. On the fateful day that Thoko finally gave in, Mother had wandered behind the servants' quarters to look at her patch of covo. She had heard the unmistakable sounds of people engaged in torrid sex. She fumed at the thought that Thoko had the nerve to bring in one of her boyfriends and she had burst, without warning, into Thoko's room. There on the narrow bed lay a naked Caleb, with a naked Thoko on top of him. Mother had let out a blood-curdling scream as though someone had stabbed her. She pounced on Thoko and pummeled the cowering girl with her fists, intent on killing her with her bare hands. By the time Tawanda got to the room, Caleb was fully clothed and he flew out though the open door, leaving Thoko to her fate at the hands of his irate mother. Tawanda was only six at the time and, when his mother realized that he was standing at the door, she stopped beating Thoko and quickly dragged him outside. Looking back, he realized that he had probably saved her life.

'Tawanda, my child, you see how women can be so evil. Imagine making a small boy like Caleb do unspeakable things to her. She is a devil! Poor Caleb…'

This was the first time Tawanda realized that, to his mother, Caleb was helpless and vulnerable.

As Tawanda grew older, he overheard people in the neighborhood talking in whispers about how he and Caleb had different fathers and how Caleb was favoured because MaNgwenya had loved his father passionately. MaNgwenya was a businesswoman, who was respected by all and feared to some degree. She travelled to Zambia, Botswana and South Africa to purchase goods to resell in Bulawayo. She lived alone with her two boys in a house, which she had extended by building three extra rooms, and which now resembled those homes in the suburbs where rich people lived. Everyone in Mzilikazi knew never to mess with her boys, particularly Caleb. He was under constant surveillance, watched by the area thugs who were paid by his mother to keep an eye out for him.

Tawanda was not a bad looking boy; however, juxtaposed with Caleb, his light visibly waned. He was shorter than his elder brother, with adolescent acne that made him self-conscious. His nose was a tad too big for his narrow face and he had close-set eyes that gave him a hawk-like expression. It did not help that he was rather quiet, but not in a menacing way or a way that made people uncomfortable around him.

As they grew up, Tawanda had never questioned his position relative to Caleb. In all families, there is a hierarchy and he was aware of this fact, and accepted his position in the pecking order. However, resentment began to build up when he noticed that there was a clear distinction between the demonstrative, caring affection Caleb received from MaNgwenya and the perfunctory, if not brusque, treatment that was Tawanda's lot. It seemed MaNgwenya loved Caleb more than him and he made a concerted effort to do everything in his power to earn her love by putting up with Caleb's excesses over the years and always bailing him out when his mother asked. However, the love and affection he craved never came. Now here he sat on a flight to go home and try to rescue Caleb. This would be his last attempt, his last major effort, mother-love notwithstanding.

Finally, after a long uncomfortable night under the cold blowing air conditioning that left him with a dry throat and burning eyes, he arrived at O. R. Tambo International Airport. He had to hurry to catch his connecting flight to Bulawayo on the other side of the airport terminal. His cousin Mbongeni was to pick him up at the airport in Bulawayo; Tawanda had an important issue to discuss with him so he had asked him to come alone.

Mbongeni was a thug and proud of it. He looked a veritable rogue, with bloodshot eyes, tobacco blackened lips and a raised scar that decorated his left cheek. Rumour had it that he had acquired the scar in a knife duel with an ex-ZANLA combatant named Lizwe, who had roamed the streets of Mpopoma, Barbourfields and Mzilikazi terrorizing people into giving him their money and property. He claimed he had fought for their liberation in the bush war and they owed him. Divesting people of their possessions was just collecting his pension. Lizwe had made the mistake of challenging Mbongeni, a perpetually angry and volatile individual who needed very little persuasion to fight. The story was that Mbongeni had slit Lizwe's throat and, along with the other spectators, had watched him bleed to death. Lizwe had been a menace, detested and feared by all. Not even his gruesome death could soften people's hearts to report Mbongeni to the police. Everyone who had been present refused to talk when they came asking questions, and the police did not force the issue. It was good riddance.

Tawanda stepped out into the bright Bulawayo sunshine. The weather was a welcome change from the dull, grey, damp conditions he had left behind in Scotland. He felt a small pang of happiness as he considered that at least he would have warm, bright November weather to enjoy while he sorted out the business about Caleb.

Mbongeni waved from a sleek, black Lexus, which was parked directly in front of a 'No Parking' sign up against the pavement. A uniformed security guard watched him, scowling and probably feeling impotent to do anything about the thug who was clearly flouting the law.

'Hey Cuz! Welcome to the place of slaughter!' Mbongeni shouted, and a group of tourists who were exiting the airport looked a little alarmed at such a welcome. 'Usharp Cuz?'

Tawanda gave his cousin a hug. He was genuinely happy to see him, despite the slight embarrassment he felt due to his unabashed loudness.

'Yebo Cuz, ngiyaphila spoks! Wena ke?' responded Tawanda. 'It was a long cold flight, otherwise not too bad.'

Mbongeni took his bag from him and threw it on the back seat of the new-smelling car. 'Let's head home bro! Umasalu is waiting for you. She is anxious. And you need to see Caleb for yourself. It's terrible man! There is a big gaping hole in his leg!' Mbongeni shuddered in revulsion. Tawanda was surprised to see such squeamishness in his tough cousin. Maybe he was getting soft with age.

'Bongi, dude, we are not going home just yet. I need to brief you on something. I am here on a mission.'

Mbongeni looked puzzled. 'Mission? What kind of mission?'

'Can you organize some of your fiercest looking buddies? Like Thambo and Felix and maybe two others?' Tawanda settled into the plush passenger's seat and looked ahead as he struggled with his seatbelt.

'Let's head out and look around for the guys. But your mother is waiting for you at home, so we need to hurry up,' Mbongeni answered as he drove slowly on to the Bulawayo Airport Road headed towards the city centre. He made a couple of calls and, while he spoke on the cell-phone, Tawanda took in the familiar sights of Bulawayo. It amazed him how things did not seem to change. The same potholes that he had seen years before were still there, only enlarged. The jacaranda trees were in their full purple regalia and the tall green elephant grass threatened to engulf the road along which the Lexus glided towards the city centre. The ramshackle buildings on the outskirts of Woodville were still standing, leaning against one another like old drunkards leaving a beer garden. The plots of land were verdant with succulent maize plants reaching upwards. Tufts of pale grey clouds littered the resplendent blue sky, holding the promise of rain showers if the heat persisted. Tawanda recalled the relief that people in Bulawayo experienced when the rains came at the predicted time. Rainfall in Matabeleland was erratic, unpredictable and long drought periods were common. Tawanda remembered the water rationing measures imposed by the Bulawayo City Council, the bucket baths and prohibition of watering of gardens using a hosepipe. He experienced that old sense of comfort and reassurance as his eyes feasted on the fertile landscape. There would be food and sufficient water this year.

A couple of hours later, Mbongeni pulled up outside Tawanda's childhood home. As he reached into the back seat to retrieve the bag, Tawanda's mother, MaNgwenya, walked out of the front door, squinting into the bright sunshine and shading her eyes with her hand. 'Bongi, what took you so long? I was beginning to get worried,' she demanded, irritably.

'The flight was delayed, Mama,' came the glib lie from Tawanda's smiling lips.

MaNgwenya walked gingerly towards Tawanda, the sun-kissed gravel on the driveway burning her bare feet. She hugged him close. He noted how fragile his mother was, in contrast to the robust full-figured woman he has left so many years ago. She was still beautiful but there were lines chiselled into her forehead and around her mouth. MaNgwenya had aged and with age had come a softness that was alien to Tawanda. Tears formed transparent pools in his eyes. MaNgwenya held him at arm's length and searched his features for physical evidence of his proclaimed wellness.

She felt a pang of guilt as she looked at her son. She had treated her two boys differently as they grew up. She had been aware of this but had been unable to fight the impulse to be over-protective of the one who was weaker. She knew she could have shown more care, given more attention to Tawanda, but it had been difficult for her. Her strength lay in loving the weak. She had failed to love his dad because he had proved to be a strong man. Weakness in her men assuaged her need to be strong and in control. Caleb's father, on the other hand, had been just like Caleb, weak of character and quite happy for her to be the dominant partner. Until he started to feel stifled and he slipped out of her vice-like grip one night, never to return. Then, she had turned all her attention to Caleb, who would always be emotionally and financially dependent on her. For a time, this was how she wanted it. However, she had created a monster for whom she now felt contempt. She looked towards the veranda of the house where Caleb lay on a hammock, with the gaping wound on his shin exposed to the breeze.

'Mama, you look exhausted. Are you well?' asked Tawanda, fear seeping slowly into his bones.

Before MaNgwenya could respond, there came a string of raspy questions, rapidly fired from the veranda. 'Mama. Is that Tawanda? Has he arrived? Is that his fine car? Mama, answer me!'

MaNgwenya sighed as she dragged Tawanda towards the voice. Mbongeni tapped Tawanda on the shoulder and whispered, 'Seven a.m. sharp tomorrow?'

Tawanda nodded imperceptibly and gave a confirmatory thumbs up.

'Mama, I have to leave now. I will be back tomorrow to pick up Tawanda for an early errand. I need his help with a project I am working on.' Mbongeni got into his car and waved as he reversed out of the short driveway.

Caleb leaned out of his hammock and pain shot through his leg. He bit down on his tongue so he would not howl in agony. He looked on as his mother approached with Tawanda, holding his hand and talking intimately.

'She's suddenly come to life, and he seems too happy,' he thought angrily. As Tawanda and his mother climbed the step onto the cool veranda, Caleb gazed at them balefully as toxic rage brewed silently inside him. He plastered a false smile onto his face. 'Tawanda, little brother.' He made as if to stand up but grimaced in pain as he fell back into the hammock. 'Sorry I couldn't come to meet you at the airport. As you can see, I am not exactly mobile.' He attempted a smile again, as he meaningfully glanced at the raw wound on his leg.

118

Tawanda crossed the short distance between them and leaned down to give his brother a hug. His nostrils were assailed by the smell of rotting flesh and he felt the contents of his stomach gurgling their way up his oesophagus. He straightened quickly before he retched over Caleb and smiled widely to mask his queasiness.

'It's good to see you too brother,' over-enthused Tawanda. 'I am sorry about your illness. I am here now and we will take care of it.'

Caleb looked pathetic in a dirty white singlet and khaki shorts. He was gaunt, his skin stretched taut over the contours of his face. He now had a full beard like the other male members of his newfound church, the Apostles of Johannes. His head was clean-shaven and seemed to wobble on his thin neck. There was a crusty whiteness around the rim of his mouth as though he had forgotten to rinse off the toothpaste after brushing his teeth. He saw himself reflected in Tawanda's gaze of pity and he hated him for it. He hated life in general now and he hoped that Tawanda would be named the source of his afflictions. That way he would have sufficient reason to despise him openly.

'I hope you brought the money we need for my healing,' Caleb wheedled and smiled a sickly fawning smile. 'You are my only hope, my brother, my last hope, otherwise I will die.'

'You will not die, my son!' MaNgwenya stated vehemently, as though speaking the words authoritatively would send death scuttling back into the shadows. However, her eyes betrayed her worst fear and her biggest hope, so she did not look at Caleb's face.

For a while, MaNgwenya and her two sons shared a heavy silence. Each of them was held in the privacy of their own thoughts, eyes downcast to keep those thoughts from one another. To reveal the nature of their thoughts would be to destroy the feeble bond of family that for so long they had kept intact by the masks they wore.

Mbongeni arrived promptly at 7 o'clock the next morning. It promised to be another pleasantly warm day.

'Hi, Scottish fella! How was your first night back in good old Zim?' Mbongeni was clearly excited about the mission at hand. He loved an adventure and this one held a particular thrill because he had a score to settle with one of the members of the Apostles of Johannes Church. He abhorred their practice of marrying young girls to wizened old men who already had multiple wives. He was particularly bitter about the marriage of his younger sister's best friend, with whom he had fallen in love. Men like him were not supposed to believe in love and he still did not quite know how it happened. One day his sister Nomsa had come home from school a blubbery mess of tears. His girl, Makanaka, whom he had never actually told about his feelings, had been pulled out of school and was being prepared for marriage to an elder in the Apostles Church for an undisclosed sum. Nomsa had tried to see her at home but she had been sent away and told never to come back.

Today was the day he, Mbongeni, would exact his revenge.

'Hi Bongi. Are the boys ready?' Tawanda was dressed in simple blue jeans and a black T-shirt. He wore a black baseball cap and aviator sunglasses making his face inscrutable as he rolled down the car window.

'Yebo, yes boss. We are going to pick them up now.'

They headed onto Sixth Avenue Extension. Tawanda took in the sights of the township. Vendors with baskets of vegetables and fruit on their heads, men on their bicycles riding towards the city centre, women with babies on their backs, young girls in skin tight jeans and half tops, boys and girls in school uniforms all made up the vibrant landscape of which he had once been a part. As they sped past the road to Mpilo Hospital on towards Renkini long distance bus terminal, Tawanda felt a pang of nostalgia. They drove past St. Patrick's Catholic Primary School, his alma mater. Tawanda was jolted out of his reverie when Mbongeni swerved to avoid a pedestrian who had wandered onto the road without checking to see if it was safe to cross over to the other side.

'Futsek stupid woman!' yelled an infuriated Mbongeni out of his window. 'Watch where you are going. Chicken brain! Nxa!'

'Easy, Bongs,' Tawanda said soothingly.

Mbongeni made a sharp right turn into the narrow entrance to the bus terminal, honking his horn furiously. Like a flock of wild geese startled by a hyena, people scattered in all directions. He screeched to a halt in front of a group of sinister-looking, muscle-bound, tattooed men. The four of them leaned casually on a large steel drum whose top served as a counter top for small bottles of brandy, with a tin can for an ashtray. Bloodshot eyes gazed languidly into the windscreen of the car and the men made no effort to move. Mbongeni opened his door and shouted, 'Eitha Majida!' pumping the air with a fist.

The men greeted him back raucously and made their way towards the car, drinks in hand.

'Boys, meet my brother Tawaz! He's a homie from abroad. Pesheya eScotland!' Mbongeni introduced his cousin.

The men shook Tawanda's hand firmly with the double pump reserved for those who were truly welcome. 'Siyakubona mScottish!' The respect they accorded him was based solely on his kinship to Mbongeni, who was clearly the alpha male.

There was a group of women standing at a distance. They looked like over-decorated Christmas trees, making eyes unabashedly at Mbongeni and his crew. All of them were dressed in second skin jeans with strategic holes carved out in the fabric to create a flesh-and-denim-coloured mosaic. The tops were cropped to reveal pert navels and alluring cleavage. One of the women deliberately dropped her eyeliner onto the ground. Then, for full effect, she stared pointedly at the group of men, slowly bent over to pick it up and peered from her head-down position to see if she had aroused any interest. One of the men whistled at the overt invitation, but Mbongeni was already starting the car. They all jumped in and Mbongeni blew the women a kiss as he drove by. They all laughed when the cute butter-coloured one showed them the middle finger.

'Ok guys, do we have all we need?' barked Mbongeni above the loud kwaito music blasting from his Bose system.

'Yes baas!' responded the men, all four of them squeezed into the back. They sat staggered to fit onto the seat: one sat forward and the next sat further back and so on, alternating to create sufficient space.

Tawanda felt a rush of adrenalin as he thought about what they were about to do. He glanced out at the blur of vegetation and human beings as they sped towards the Umguza River, where the Apostles of Johannes were meeting for their all-day Saturday worship. As they drove along the road, swerving to avoid potholes and pedestrians, the boys in the back seat sang along to the music; 'That'isgubhu, us'fak' ezozweni, ufak' amaspecs uzobuzwa ubunand' obulapha!' This was the refrain to a popular South African hit extolling the pleasures of home-brewed beer. Tawanda tapped his foot to the heavy beat and reached back for a small bottle of brandy. It landed in his palm and he took a quick swig. He let the molten brew sit in his mouth for a few seconds, then savoured its searing descent down his gullet and into his stomach; from there it radiated waves of heat slowly to his limbs and to his head. Tawanda was suddenly riding on a wave of euphoria to be home in Bulawayo. He felt like he was one of these men, Mbongeni, Sakhile, Mzingaye, Felix and Thambo, who had accepted him in their midst without any suspicion. They did not even seem to notice that he had a Shona name and, if they did, it seemed to be of no consequence to them. He was a Bulawayo boy, raised by an Ndebele mother and that is all that mattered. The nature of the other half of his genetic makeup was neither here nor there.

Then they saw it. To the left was a huge clearing upon which flowed a sea of white-clad human beings. To one side was a large group of men clad in green robes, with shaven heads and long beards. All of them carried crooked staffs. All in all, there must have been over 400 people gathered in the clearing on the bank of the river. The sound of the engine in the relatively quiet place attracted the attention of the throng and many turned their heads towards the car.

The men spilled out of the car and Mbongeni and Tawanda casually walked towards the clearing. They tried to look as non-threatening as possible, bowing slightly to the elder who came to meet them. Elder Moses quickly took in the jet-black Lexus with tinted windows and the attire of the men approaching him. He pasted his public relations smile on to his face. He could smell money. Stopping directly in front of the men, he addressed them in his most authoritative voice, 'Greetings, in the name of our Lord, the highest God, my children. I see you are here on a higher mission. Speak, God is listening!' He closed his eyes and mumbled unintelligible prayers.

Tawanda and Mbongeni stepped forward and bowed reverentially before Elder Moses. They had decided that Mbongeni would do all the talking.

'Please sir, we would like to speak with Prophet Daniel. It is about our brother Caleb Ngwenya from Mzilikazi, who is severely ill. I believe if you mention the name Caleb, he will understand.'

Elder Moses knew of this case and asked, 'And who shall I say is here, my children?'

'Please tell him it is the younger brother from overseas,' replied Mbongeni, injecting some meekness into his voice.

Elder Moses' insides did a dance of glee. He was right, here was money. A whole lot of it.

'Very well, my children, wait here.'

Prophet Daniel, flanked by two other bearded men, walked towards them at a brisk but controlled pace. Elder Moses brought up the rear. As they got closer and their facial features became distinguishable, Mbongeni muttered explosively, 'Well, son of a gun! If it isn't the cradle-robbing paedophile himself! Shit!'

Tawanda turned to him and whispered 'What? Who are you talking about?'

'That Daniel character is the bearded gnome that my Makanaka was married off to. Oh, this is going to turn out to be more fun than I had imagined!'

'Easy Bongi, let's play it cool so as to not mess up the mission. Here they come, shhh!' Tawanda and Mbongeni straightened up to face the oncoming group of green-garbed men.

Prophet Daniel and his group were within arm's reach, all effusive smiles and sickly charm. Mbongeni glanced over their shoulders at the masses in the clearing and noted that they were all preoccupied with their rituals. A leader had started a song and they were singing full throttle. Perfect. Mbongeni gave a subtle signal to the men by the car and the four of them marched towards them. The Apostles looked a little startled by the approach of the burly men to whom they had not paid much attention. The six men encircled the Apostles and drew their pistols. There was a clattering sound and audible gasps as the Apostles let go their holy staffs, which fell to the ground. They spontaneously held up their hands in a gesture of surrender.

'Pick your damn sticks up right now and put your hands down or I will blow your heads off!' Mbongeni snarled.

The terrified men bent to pick up their staffs and two of them bumped heads in their haste to get back into the upright position.

Tawanda kept his pistol to his side while he spoke. 'Gentlemen, we are peaceful men and so we want to resolve a very important issue without undue bloodshed. Caleb is my elder brother and I hear that he has refused to go to the hospital to get treatment for his rotting leg because you have told him that his wound is due to a spiritual curse. You, Prophet Daniel, are the main architect of the whole fiasco because you are the prophet who gave him that message. OK. I am listening. Tell me the prophecy in your own words.'

Emboldened by the civilized manner in which Tawanda spoke, Prophet Daniel started to speak. He had to raise his voice because the singing in the background had increased in volume and intensity, and the white-robed women had formed a circle and were shuffling, three steps to the left and three to the right. A cloud of dust billowed from the ground upwards like an offering of incense.

'My son,' he began. 'I saw a vision when your brother first came to me and, in this vision, there was a dark cloud that followed him wherever he went. He ate and slept with this cloud over him and everything he touched turned to worms.'

Prophet Daniel licked his lips nervously and looked around to gauge the effect of his delivery. He swallowed hard and continued, 'Then the dark cloud started to cast an even darker shadow over him. It was the shadow of death and he started to shrink a little every day. Then Elder Joshua here interpreted the vision.'

Elder Joshua glared at Prophet Daniel.

'Go on, Elder Joshua,' prompted Tawanda. 'Continue please. What was the meaning of that vision?'

'Well, I heard a voice in my head, the voice of God, telling me that the cloud was a curse and that each passing day the curse would cause more and more calamity until he eventually died a hideous death. The worms, I was told, were a sign that someone in his family had placed the curse and taken all his luck. The person would benefit directly from Caleb's work, while Caleb's health would deteriorate.'

'And did the voice tell you who this wicked relative usurping Caleb's luck was?' asked Tawanda, blowing into the barrel of his pistol.

Elder Joshua paused a second too long. Mbongeni placed the barrel of his pistol against his temple and whispered, 'Speak, you old fool!'

'Y- yes, the voice said it was a very close relative,' whined the elder.

'Who, dammit?' demanded Mbongeni, kicking him forcefully on the left shin.

His leg buckled and he wailed, 'His younger brother! The one who lives abroad! That is how he is so successful while his elder brother sinks deeper into penury. Ouch!' He limped as he tried to stand on the left leg.

'OK. That's enough of this nonsense! You charlatans have messed with the wrong family this time and I want you to listen very well.' Tawanda spoke with a menacing calm, looking with cool contempt at the group of peasant-looking men.

'Here is a new prophesy, which you will deliver first thing tomorrow morning without fail. You will go to Caleb's house, the four of you, and you will tell Caleb in the presence of his mother that God has said he needs to go to the hospital at once. You will also tell him that his younger brother has nothing to do with his failures and that he needs to stop making excuses for his own failings. You will tell him that he needs to get a job as soon as he is well or else God will send him a death so painful he will continue to feel the pain long after he has been buried.

'Your message to his mother is that she must stop treating a grown man as though he were a small boy. You will tell her that, six months after he has recovered, she is to send him out of her home or else both will perish in an unquenchable fire of unknown origin.'

Tawanda continued, 'You will stop extorting money for miracles from innocent people, who go on to die thanks to your trickery and discouragement from seeking medical attention. You will stop child abuse and stop this evil practice of marrying children young enough to be your granddaughters!'

At this, Mbongeni stepped towards Prophet Daniel and pointed his gun to his ribs. 'That goes for you sickko! Makanaka will be at her parents' house by 3 p.m. this afternoon so help you God! And if you or your sick friends are seen anywhere within a hundred metres of her, I will personally visit you with enough bullets for each member of your household and all your animals! I have warned you!'

'Alright then, this meeting is adjourned,' Tawanda pronounced. 'Enjoy the rest of your service and remember, there are eyes and ears everywhere.'

As the four Apostles backed away, too scared to turn around in case they got shot in the back, the friends flashed their pistols one more time as they withdrew towards their car. They roared with laughter as they watched the thin wiry men in their long green robes hurtling towards their multitudes as though a thousand hounds were nipping at their heels.

As they piled back into the car they glanced across the flat riverbank at the dancing congregation who were totally oblivious to what had just taken place. They would be told that God had sent a message and they would simply comply.

Tawanda felt liberated and, for the first time in years, he believed there would be a turnaround in his family. He glanced at his watch and was surprised to find that it was only nine thirty. The whole mission had taken a little over two hours. Now he could totally relax and enjoy his week in Bulawayo. No visit to konthuthu ziyathunqa, the place of billowing smoke, as Bulawayo was known, would be complete without a visit to the famous MaDlodlo Bar.

The Lexus flew down the busy street, with the passengers singing along to Brenda Fassie's hot song Vulindlela. They stopped by a roadside vendor to buy roasted maize and carried on driving around trying to decide where to go and spend the rest of their day before going to MaDlodlo's later.

Self-Portrait

Bongani Kona

1.

Life, as I understand it now, is an attempt to right some quarrel with our parents. My father is dead – heart attack, many years ago now – and buried on a small of patch of land in rural Musengezi, but we haven't ceased fighting.

2.

How to begin. I am an apprentice writer, and, suppose like all beginning writers, my stories are molded from autobiography. I'm tempted to disguise the animus between my father and me in fiction, in a semi-autobiographical short story, say, with convincing dialogue, exposition and scenes. To achieve, I think, the right measure of distance.

And yesterday I made a start:

February 1997[1]; a miserably hot summer evening. Here I am. Backstage on opening night. Dressed in a salmon-pink nightdress, revealing a pair of stringy arms and scrawny legs. I've been cast as Linda, Willy Loman's loyal wife, in my high school's production of *Death of a Salesman*. Hubert – or perhaps I should call him my husband? – stands a breath away

---

[1] The year is significant for two reasons. In real-life I started high school that year, at Prince Edward, and that summer, coincidentally, Canaan Sodindo Banana, the country's first president, was arrested on charges of sodomy. At my school, it was commonplace to refer to young boys like myself, thought to be too effeminate, as 'Sodindo.'

127

from me. Our hands brush in the semidarkness. Something pulses between us. My skin tingles.

The curtains part. A solid bar of yellow light falls upon the stage. Act 1. Scene 1. Enter stage left. Willy! I shout in a ridiculous high-pitched voice. Is that you? Laughter ripples through the auditorium. Through the corner of my eye I see my father, in his army fatigues. Seated with my mother in the middle of the third row. His brows gather into deep furrows.

3.

Families like ours, neither bad nor good, just imperfect, are held together not so much by secrets but silences. What I have then is a compulsion to lay out the facts, to hold everything up to the light.

4.

My mother, religious to the point of mania, died shortly after my father. The name Bongani ('give thanks') had been her idea. I was born six weeks early, at Mbuya Nehanda Maternity Hospital, in October '85. When she saw me in the neonatal ward, breathing through a tangle of tubes, as the story goes, she had a vision of Daniel walking through King Nebuchadnezzar's furnace with the Angel of the Lord. Then she heard Daniel say, Give thanks to the Lord, for he is good, for his mercy endures forever.

5.

We lived in a three-bedroomed house on a narrow expanse of street, shaded with gum trees, in a former whites-only neighbourhood in the south of Harare. I had a standard upbringing for an only child – periods of sustained boredom and idleness alleviated only by watching cartoons on ZBC. My parents were what you might call straightforward – in the Zimbabwean sense of the word. By that I mean they were old fashioned, not the kind of people that will surprise you any. My father was a mid-ranking military officer, stationed at the Cranborne Barracks, and my mother worked as a senior administrator at Cairns Foods.

On Sundays, we drove my father's green Peugeot 504 to the church with a red brick façade in Msasa Park, Apostles of Christ Ministries, where he sometimes preached to the congregation. When I think of those Sundays – I no longer go to church – I see my father standing behind the pulpit. Dressed in a navy blue suit, a stern look in his eyes. Mimicking the gestures of our second president. How he sometimes raises a clenched fist for emphasis.

And it's always the same sermon. The one where he gives an etymology of the word deacon. He says, deacon, from the Greek, diakonos, which means to serve.

6.

You're writing again, Tongai says, lighting a cigarette. Plumes of blue-grey smoke curl up into the ochre sunset. You seem more relaxed when you're writing. Less tense.

We're sitting outside Cocoa Wah Wah, a sidewalk café in Rondebosch. Tongai is one of a handful of Zimbabwean friends I have here. We met in the winter, some years ago now, in a bar on Trill Road, Tagore's, a bohemian hangout which swarmed with beautiful faces and had that musky old furniture smell. It was Friday night and the band was playing a cover of Mingus' 'Gunslinging Bird', when Tongai walked in, dressed in a black coat with tails and a red woollen scarf draped over his shoulders.

He stood almost a head taller than everyone in that tiny bar and he had what I think of as a traveller's face: earnest and alert. I watched him take off his scarf, folding it over the upturned palm of his left hand, and our eyes met, and he smiled. A crooked, sideways kind of smile.

So, are you going to tell me what it's about?

You know how, in *House of Hunger*, Marechera tells the story of how his father died three times, I say. Three times and it's different each time. When I was younger I was obsessed with telling apart the truth from fiction. Now, I see it doesn't matter. Doesn't matter at all. It's like how some musicians return to the same refrain over and over, I'm interested in that. This always returning. Not the quote-unquote real story.

7.

I met Hubert Chipangura in the winter of 1996, when the Van De Ruits, an elderly white couple with no children, moved out of Elmore Street. The rambling double storey house they'd lived in was taken over by the Chipanguras; a family with two sons, both tall and reedy, and Hubert, the youngest of the pair, was my age. We grew closer as friends after he was transferred to Widdecombe Primary School at the start of the second term and placed in my class, 6 Red.

The other kids in the class thought he was funny looking – Hubert's face was nearly all pimples and he had comically large ears – and children being what they are, unable to hide their cruelty, stayed away from him.

8.

What are you doing? I said.

I had walked over to Hubert's desk during break-time, when it was only the two of us left in the classroom. The wooden desks were arranged in neat rows, facing the blackboard. Hubert's desk was closer to the front, in the middle of the second row. He sat with his back hunched over an A4 piece of paper.

Nothing, he said, sticking out his tongue and moving to cover the piece of paper with his right arm.

Wait, wait! he said, when I pulled on the paper and it threatened to tear. I'll show you... if you promise not to tell anyone.

I stood motionless, held in a trance by what was on the paper. Outside, I could hear the clamour of voices and the faint hum of a lawn mower.

Um. I saw it in a movie, Hubert said.

The drawing, you could see, was the work of someone skilled. The suppleness of the woman's breasts, the tautness of the man's muscles, the overall balance of light and shade.

(*In the dream I had that night, in which I woke up feeling ashamed, crying, the man was crouched over the woman's mid-section, his hands cupped over her breasts.*)

9.

This afternoon, deciding to stretch my legs, I ventured into a second-hand bookshop in Observatory. Browsing the shelves, I read about a South American writer – I forget his name now – who had dedicated his debut collection of stories to his best friend, Eduardo: *with all my love*. A decade later, when the book was reissued by a big North American publisher, he declined all requests to write a foreword.

Instead, he asked if could change the dedication. To Eduardo, he wrote, *with all my hate*.

I can understand that, how easily feelings can shift from love to hate. Or vice versa.

10.

We had a housekeeper, Rosemary – thin, high cheekbones, braided hair, and always wore black tennis shoes – who worked three days a week. And so Tuesday and Thursday afternoons I spent unsupervised, watching cartoons on the television set in the living room, though my parents expected me to be studying.

One afternoon, after we'd walked the winding stretch of road from Widdecombe, I asked Hubert if we could watch the movie with the drawings.

Hubert said, I can't show it to anyone.

We argued back and forth, at low intensity – we were in Elmore Street now – until Hubert relented. I waited outside the spiked black gate to our house as Hubert ran to go and retrieve the VHS tape from its hiding place.

11.

I don't recall now what the film was about, its narrative thread. That whole afternoon is condensed into a state of feeling – of heat rising, skin tingling, shallow intakes of breath – brought on by seeing bodies on the cathode screen in various stages of undress. I don't remember, too, what transpired before Hubert and I found ourselves rolling around on the grey carpet.

Now picture this: your mother walks into a dimly-lit living room, animated by Godless sounds, to find her eleven-year old son, still in his school khakis, kissing the neighbour's pimply-faced boy.

12.

I never saw Hubert again. He was packed off to a boarding school somewhere and his parents moved from Elmore Street a
year later. With the passage of years, life took on its own rhythm and I had all but forgotten about him until that winter night, many years later, when I met Tongai.

13.

Brrr. It's cold, Tongai said, warming his cupped hands with his breath. What are you drinking?

Wine.

Hmm. I need something stronger, he said, reaching into the pocket of his coat to pull out a clump of creased bank notes, and a key ring with a fluffy tiger. The rims of his fingernails, I saw, as he flattened the bank notes on the mahogany-coloured counter, were caked with paint.

Just as I thought to ask him where he was from, the bar ruptured into applause when the trumpeter, face glazed with sweat, reached the end of his solo.

So, I said, moments later when it quietened down, where you from?

That's a political question, he said. Laughing.

No, no, no, I said, surprised by the tinge of panic in my voice. I mean, you sound like you're from Zim. You look like someone I used to know. That's all.

We were sitting almost a metre apart now, on the cushioned bar stools, and Tongai turned to look at me, his face coming into focus in the dim crimson light. I hadn't noticed until now but his eyes were a different colour, brown and solid black, skewing the symmetry of his face.

Listen, he said, reaching for my arm. Can you hear that?

Coltrane?

Yeah, yeah. Pay attention. The mood... the different strokes... the textures. It's like... a painting.

He had his eyes closed now. As the band played on, he shifted his hand from my arm and slipped it underneath my shirt, reaching for the small of my back. I sipped the half-empty wine glass and I could hear myself swallow.

Tongai stood up and drained his drink.

Follow me, he said.

I obeyed his instruction, following behind his solid mass threading through the press of bodies. He waited for me to enter the bathroom and he cast a wide glance across the bar before bolting the wooden door.

He craned his neck to kiss me. A soft, gentle kiss that nearly made me weep with desire.

14.

Here then, is what truly happened. In the summer of 1997, the year Canaan Sodindo Banana was arrested on charges of sodomy, and he appeared nightly on the 8 o'clock News surrounded by a phalanx of reporters and bodyguards, I was cast in the school's production of *Twelfth Night*. And much to the disappointment of my father – sending me to an all-boys boarding school was meant to straighten me out, a remedy of sorts – I played Viola, a woman pretending to be a man.

Every time I appeared on stage, on opening night, a soft chorus rose up from the back of the auditorium where the other boarding school boys were seated: *Sodindo, Sodindo, Sodindo!* (And for this they would be roundly castigated at the next assembly by the headmaster, Mr. Davis, for embarrassing the school by behaving like a bunch of savages.)

By the time I delivered my favourite lines –

Viola: *We men may say more, swear more, but indeed*
Our shows are more than will, for still we prove
Much in our vows, but little in our love.

Orsino: *But died thy sister of her love, my boy?*

Viola: *I am all the daughters of my father's house,*
And all the brothers too – and yet I know not.

my father had left the auditorium. I wept uncontrollably on stage looking at the two empty seats.

I have never been on stage since, and, suppose, neither have I stopped weeping.

15.

The buzzer to my first-floor apartment emits a loud whine. Let me in, Tongai says over the intercom. I brought wine... and lentils!

The latch on the gate unhinges. I hear the sound of Tongai's footsteps rushing up the flight of stairs. He is dressed in black denims and combat boots stained with paint.

Is the story finished? I thought you might like something to eat... I made rice and lentils.

16.

I still remember the first time Tongai and I slept together. Back then, he lived in a two-bedroom semi just across from the train tracks in

Observatory and his room – cluttered with canvasses, paints, sketch pads, a stack of vinyls and a black record player stashed in the corner – had a sky view. He was still studying to be a painter at the arts campus on Orange Street and I was a third year English major with dreams of becoming a writer.

I liked to read before sex and that winter we read from some of the writers in my Contemporary Fiction Syllabus. Alice Munro ('Royal Beatings'), Harold Brodkey ('Innocence'), Jhumpa Lahiri ('A Temporary Matter'), David Bezmozgis, ('Natasha'), Junot Díaz ('How To Date A Brown Girl (black girl, white girl, or halfie)').

That afternoon, I read Stacy Hardy's 'My Black Lover'. Both of us were naked, the room bathed in winter-grey sunlight, and Tongai had his arms around me, his chin kneading the muscles on my shoulder. Afterwards, when we lay on our backs with our legs entangled, I remember thinking how what we shared felt real and beautiful and everlasting.

And so it was.

17.

I'm just going to warm this up, Tongai says, kissing me on the cheek. You finish up. I won't disturb.

Don't worry, I'm nearly done.

Ah, he says, then you can tell me what it's all about. But only after you give me a hand washing the dishes, geez, do you even have one clean utensil here Mr B?

18.

My one-bedroom apartment faces the main street in Rosebank. Outside, the sky is nearly black and, in the distance, I can hear the sound of the last train leaving the station.

Jericho

Adrian Fairbairn

That night in camp I turn in early, my chest tight and agitated. The others are five beers ahead, and I am in no mood to play catch-up. I received a barracking for leaving them again, but I cannot get my thoughts away from Jericho and the Sleeping Pool. What he had asked was an honour, though I have no way of knowing if I can deliver...

Travis Williams (Will), 48. Certified member of IANTD (International Association of Nitrox and Technical Divers). Professional diving instructor with 22 years experience. At odds with his wife and society in general. Has an affinity for beer.

Markus Dowerman, 46. Certified IANTD member, 15 years diving experience. Investment banker. Single. Alimony payments, a wandering eye and a wicked sense of humour.

Tim Roberts, 28. Certified IANTD member, 6 years diving experience. The baby of the group. Happily married with Tim Junior on the way. Boyish good looks but eyes that show a maturity beyond his years.

Jack Roberts, 50. Widower and business owner, as well as devoted father of Tim. Manager and financial backer of our little excursion.

Gavin Stone, 47. Me. Certified member of IANTD with 17 years diving experience. A family that means the world to me. A very undistinguished business career. This is to be my final dive.

Will, Markus, Jack and I are all alumni of Plumtree High. The others left the country after school, worried about the propects in the newly formed Zimbabwe. I stayed on and rode out the years, jumping from business to business as the tough times hit. The group kept in touch and once a year we met at a pre-selected dive site to rekindle our friendship.

I watch Will, Markus and Jack as their conversation floats from our early years in Zimbabwe, the school rivalries, the women of our past, and then to diving. Always a full circle back to diving. Their voices go up with excitement as the subject comes up. Tim watches, not saying much, but he too is completely obsessed by the mistress that has captured our hearts.

Outside of family time, I think I'll miss these trips the most: the camaraderie, the banter and the shared passion that bonds us. I keep to myself the condition that will soon consume me; weaken my frame and then slowly my resolve. Still, as the dry landscape rolls by outside my window on our drive from Harare, I know to make the best of this entry on my bucket list, the 105 metre dive to the soul of the caves.

The excitement in the twin cab is palpable as Will guides the vehicle into Chinhoyi Caves National Park and up to a deserted camp site. We park to the left of the ablution blocks, under the spreading arms of a giant msasa tree. Its amber and wine-red hues in stark contrast to the faded brown of the savannah that surrounds it.

I know the way down to the caves and I am itching to go. I get a look from Will. He knows this trip is personal to me, even if he doesn't know why.

'Go Gav. We'll set up camp… just after Tim gets us a beer.'

I smile in his direction. 'Go steady, we're diving tomorrow.'

'Only 50 metres, Gav. Walk in the park,' I hear him say, my back already turned.

I make my way to the path that leads to the cave mouth. A flash pulls my attention heavenward. Clouds pregnant and moody rumble overhead.

'Better hurry,' I shout, 'rains-a-coming.' They grunt something derogatory in response.

The path is exactly as I remember it from a stop-in on the way to Chirundu in my youth. The concrete and inlaid stone path winds between the moss-covered rocks and vegetation. The first of the 288 steps comes into view, dropping down from ground level and into the gaping mouth of the cave.

It takes a second for my eyes to adjust to the dim light. I shorten my stride and pay particular attention to my footsteps. Injury before the dives would be catastrophic. An eerie stillness hangs in the cave. I hear the sound of my breathing. The occasional crunch underfoot echoes. Twice I turn around to see if I am alone.

The light increases as I near the far opening of the cave, revealing the stalactite structures of the rock above me. Five metres on, the enclosed space gives way to a vast opening: a cavern with a collapsed roof that lets in the natural light from the sky above, sheer stone walls dropping 50 metres to the blue waters of the Sleeping Pool below. It takes my breath away.

The angle of the steps grows steeper as if they too are desperate to reach the water. I slow my descent, almost in a hypnotic state, my eyes flicking between the steps and the water. I stop once to look up at what seems to be a portal to heaven. It is more than I could have wished for.

As I near the bottom where the rocks surrender to the water, I notice an old man sitting on his haunches, staring unseeing into the depths. His clothes hang lopsidedly on his skeletal frame, his face weathered and lived-in. He does not look up, does not acknowledged my presence.

'Mhoroi, baba,' I eventually say. A little embarrassed, as I often am, by my limited grasp of local languages. I have lived here long enough to know more, but never took the time.

He stirs as if coming out of a reverie. Blinking a couple of times as he focuses on me. Our conversation is stilted at first as we discuss the beauty of our surroundings and the hardships that have befallen our country. I ask him what he thinks of those who rule, those who control. His answer is sobering, 'I am not a politician, I am not well educated, my years have taught me my path. I am a child of the earth, a friend of my spirit ancestors. They guide me. But every man knows right from wrong.' It is left there.

An uneasy silence settles and only when I mention that we have come to dive to the bottom of the caves do his eyes sparkle and his smile betrays a crooked tooth line. He is silent for a long moment after that; then he speaks in a tone that cuts away the triviality of small talk and seems to give a deeper insight into the man he is.

'Our name for this place is Chirorodziva. It means Pool of the Fallen.'

Adrian Fairbairn

I sit down next to him, getting comfortable, prompting him to continue.

'An Nguni man called Nyamakwere lived on this land long ago. Long before my father and long before his father before him. Nyamakwere was a cruel man; he threw our people from the cliffs above.'

His finger comes up and points to the rock face that dwarfs us. I find myself looking up, trying to imagine the horror of being flung from such a height.

'It is believed that the pool has no floor... The water sits on the bones of the dead.'

'Is that why you're here? To pay them respect?'

A breeze comes up and the old man's clothes flap against him. He shudders and looks down but not quickly enough to disguise the tears that build up in his eyes.

'I have come to this place every day since I can remember. My children used to play near here when they were young. One day my daughter, my son and their friend ran into some drunk miners. There are a lot of miners in this area. My daughter was always scared of them. She called them 'white ghosts' because of the powder coating on their bodies from the dolomite mines. She had heard me tell stories of how our people used to use the caves to hide from the raiding tribes, so the children came here for sanctuary.' He pauses and points to a big rock to our left. 'That is where she fell from.'

I look across. The rock protrudes about three metres out of the water and has a steep, slippery-looking face. The old man falls silent, eyes closed, as if reliving the terror of the day.

'I'm sorry,' I say.

'Her brother jumped in to save her and they were both lost. Swallowed by these still waters.'

Silence looms. Words seem inadequate at this point. What can be said to soften such a devastating blow? I simply lay a hand on his frail shoulder. As if on cue, the first raindrops strike the mirror sheen of the Sleeping Pool. It is as if the sky is weeping in solidarity. I feel the old man's grip on my arm and, for the first time, he looks right at me, right into me.

'Will you help me find my children?'

I nod slowly. 'I will do what I can.'

His hand takes mine and he grins. 'Jericho, my name is Jericho.'
'Gavin,' I reply.
'Thank you, Gavin. Thank you.'

The camp is quiet when I awake the following day, the serenity broken
occasionally by snores from the tents dotted around the fire pit. I
rekindle the fire and boil water for coffee. I read a text from my wife
and reply, telling her I am feeling fine, then listen to a voice message
from my son that almost makes my heart burst. I send one back and
toss the phone into my bag at the entrance of my tent. It is going to be a
long day of preparation, so I think an hour of solitude by the Sleeping
Pool before the others awake may be the tonic. I follow the path, coffee
in hand, and again I am swallowed by the mouth of the cave.

As I wind my way down, I am struck by the colour of the pool. It is
brighter today; a rich cobalt blue that reflects the overhead sky. I am so
enchanted that it takes a while to notice Jericho, sitting in the same
position. The old man is in good spirits this morning as if buoyed by
my presence. His smile presses down heavily on my shoulders, the
pressure to find him closure is immense. He is wearing a strip of pink
fabric around his right wrist, the fingers of his left hand gently fondling
it, his eyes for a moment again lost in the pool.

'Good morning,' I say. Then, without tact, blurt out, 'Was that your
daughter's?'

He gives a weary smile and fumbles with the knot that holds the
cloth in place. Shaking it out so it changes shape, now almost square
like a handkerchief.

'If a relative dies, we give away their clothes.' He pauses,
smoothing out the fabric. 'The day my children died, I came to this
place, took soil and put it into this cloth. I took it back to my
homestead, near the Manyame River, and placed it beside my bed.'

He senses my question and holds up his hand.

'The spirits of the dead become one with the land at the place of
death. We bring them home for one last night, then the villagers get
together the following day, dig a small hole and place the soil into it. It
is how we say goodbye.'

I am horrified and intrigued at the same time. The thought of a dead
child's clothes on another child, that perhaps you could see daily, must
be so hard on a parent. But I suppose each culture has its mysteries. The

thought of having your loved one's ashes in an urn on the mantel must be equally disturbing, if not more so, to those who have not been brought up with the custom.

'So you have nothing of them, no small reminder?'

He shakes his head slowly.

'The day before my children died, my wife had come back from a trip to Harare. She had been given...' He fumbles for the word, his hands instinctively going to his wrist.

'Bracelets?' I guess.

'Yes, the ones that stretch, with beads. She gave them to the children. They probably still wear them.'

'Gav!' Will's voice echoes down to us. 'We could use some help with the gas mix.'

'On the way,' I shout back.

I walk from the pool to the first of the steps before I turn. 'What is your last name, Jericho?'

He looks up, using his hand to shield his eyes from the sun. 'Tonderai, it means to remember.'

We both smile at the irony, and I begin my trek back to camp.

The generator is purring as I reach the rest of the group. Tim and Jack have their heads down, pouring over the dive tables, while Will has taken the responsibility of blending the oxygen, nitrogen and helium in the dive tanks. The light-hearted, playful side of the men is replaced by the technical, no-nonsense aspect of our trip. There are such small margins for error: too much oxygen leads to toxicity, but too little and you run the risk of hypoxia, where a diver could lose consciousness. Excess nitrogen causes a narcotic effect, so it is easy to lose your bearings. Helium is introduced to reduce the narcotic effect but it, in turn, increases heat loss from the body. All these factors need to be carefully weighed and measured so as to create an equilibrium, and keep the diver safe.

Markus has the tanks laid out and is attaching the regulators as Will completes the mixes. The proportions of each gas have to be adjusted for the varying depths that we intend to dive.

'Are you okay, Gav?' Markus asks, as I hand him one of the regulators.

'Yeah, I'm good,' I lie.

In that intimate moment I could share everything I am going through and, as God is my witness, I want to. I could unburden myself of my illness; the bond I have created with Jericho and the pressure that comes with it; the fact that this is to be my last dive, and how much I will miss every one of them. Markus is a good enough friend to keep my fears a secret, but for some reason, I can't do it. I give an unconvincing smile; he sees right through it, but does not push the issue. He simply puts his hand on my shoulder and squeezes.

'Right then, you lazy bugger, bring the rest of the tanks and then check the radios are charged.'

Our first dive is to be on air and, later, trimix; so laden with three tanks each, regulators and our dive bags, I lead the way down. By halfway, my legs are burning from the weight. Will is close behind, breathing heavily under his load.

'Perhaps that last beer wasn't such a good idea,' he grunts.

I laugh and let him pass; my breathing is laboured too and I begin to cough from deep in my chest.

'You ok, Gav?' Will looks back at me.

'Not enough beer,' I joke, still feeling the pain in my chest.

'Seriously Gavin, are you ok?' Will's eyes are intense, the concern etched into his face.

'I'm good, Will, just give me a minute... I may be getting a bit of flu.'

It hurts me to lie to him. He holds my stare way past comfort, and then turns back towards the pool.

Tim and Markus shuffle by, brows creased in concentration, watching each footstep and every stone step tick by. My gaze follows the path up to a large mukwa tree, where Jack is leaning against its trunk. Two red-winged starlings chat in the branches above his head, and I watch as his eyes scour the canopy searching for their nest. His burden is the camera bags, tool boxes, medical kit and cooler box with the food and drink for the day.

'You good, Jack?' I yell.

I get a thumbs up, and he begins to move again. Another coughing fit grabs me. I raise a handkerchief to my mouth to silence the hacking. I shoot a glance down the incline to Will who has half turned. I see him say something to Markus, but they keep going. I revert my attention to the white cotton cloth in my hand. In its centre is a crimson stain where the blood was absorbed by the material. I curse silently, folding it and returning it to my pocket.

The water is a pleasant 23 degrees Celsius. All the divers are kitted out, at last, and in the water going through the pre-dive safety checks. Because of Will's experience, it has been decided that he will buddy Tim, which leaves me with Markus. Jericho's face holds a mixture of fascination and excitement, despite me telling him that our dive is only to 55 metres, about halfway between the surface and the bottom of the pool. He is a little standoffish with the others, but holds firm eye contact with me.

Jack is shouting instructions to Tim from a rock near where Jericho sits. The trepidation of a father, watching his son putting himself in danger, is something I never want to experience. Tim is, as always, respectful, but you can see the frustration as he rechecks his gear for the fourth time as per his father's request.

At last it is time, and we wave to the men on the bank, slowly letting out the air from our BCs as we slip under the surface of the water. My descent is slightly faster than the others, and I watch the ghostlike silhouettes above me captured by the backdrop of the sunlight behind. The feeling of freedom underwater is indescribable. Weightless, unhampered and totally at peace.

Some 20 metres down we pass a shelf that juts out from the side wall of the cavern and encroaches four metres into the pool. Tim wastes no time as he inverts himself and precedes to moonwalk backwards on the underside of the shelf. I hear Markus laughing in my ear piece. Tim's air bubbles that escape the regulator follow the shelf in search of the surface, making their way round the rock and hugging the wall. In the filtering light, they appear dense and shine bright like silver balls of mercury tumbling over each other in a race to the top.

Time passes so quickly and, before we know it, we are almost at the end of the decompression stops on our ascent. The minute our heads break the water, high fives and excited chatter begin. Everybody saw the same things but the way each describes their own experience gives a moment of reflection. Jack looks on, his face showing a mixture of relief for our safety and a tinge of jealousy that he was not part of the experience.

Jericho's look is more an appeal. I break from the group and whisper that it was the start, and things were looking good for the next day. He nods as though he understands, but his eyes show the way to a desperate soul that has waited too long.

We shed our heavy gear and share a meal with Jericho at the water's edge. The guys banter and fire questions at the old man, but he doesn't reveal the pain of his past to the others.

At dusk we start to prepare for the next dive. The extra mixed gas tanks brought down by Jack and Jericho while we were under are put in place and the checks begin again. A target depth of 75 metres is punched into our 2G dive computers and, as full darkness nears, we once again enter the water. High-powered torch beams flicker around the surrounding rocks. A startled dassie is caught in Tim's beam, frozen by the light. It eventually breaks its trance and scurries to safety in one of the many cracked rock faces. A final run through and once again we descend.

I keep close to Markus on the way down. At 15 metres we pause, looking back up to the surface of the pool. The stars in the night sky are clearly visible, it is surreal.

My chest feels tight and I cough violently; a flurry of bubbles exits the regulator, and quickly the beam of Markus's torch is on me. My communication gear crackles… 'Gav, you alright?'

I make a figure 'O' with my thumb and index finger to signal all okay, unable to speak from the fluid in my mouth, which I release out through the regulator. I can tell Markus isn't convinced.

'We need to chat about this when we get topside,' he says.

Almost immediately, Will chimes in. 'What's the problem?'

'No problem,' I reply. 'No problem at all.'

'Okay, watch your depths and gauges, we'll be at 75 metres before you know it.'

He is right, we pass 50 then 55 metres. The deeper we get, the more pressure I feel on my chest. The urge to cough is overwhelming. I keep trying to swallow to control it, and then, at 62 metres, the urge inexplicably disappears. My breathing becomes more settled and, for the first time, I begin to enjoy the dive.

An underwater cave entrance yawns in the sheer rock face, our torch beams stab at its blackness but only penetrate a few metres. Both Markus and I float towards it, as if lured by something. The hair on my body stands on end, as I sense a presence I can't explain. It is almost as if the darkness is moving. Markus must be feeling it too. His torch beam swings in a frantic arc, and the bubbles around him instantly increase. Then, for a split second, the light around us intensifies outside the brightness of our torches. I feel a warmth around my suit that dissipates as the darker state resumes.

'Did you see that?' I hear him shout.

'I felt it!' I reply, still freaked out by what I cannot explain. My heartbeat now loud in my ears.

Then, without warning, the exact feeling and sensation is repeated.

'What the f…' the words are lost behind the bubbles that rise from his regulator. 'Will, what depth are you at?'

I can hear the panic in Markus's voice.

'We're at 75 metres. Why?'

I check my gauge and we are still hovering around 63 metres.

'Something moving up here. I swear it,' Markus says.

'Are you sure?' Will does not wait for an answer. 'Get down to 75 metres and join us. It's better that we are together, then we can start making our ascent.'

It is all that we talk about as we take our stops on the way up. As we break the surface, a halo of solar lamps surrounds the pool. The volume of our voices grows and echoes as we excitedly recount the experience to Jack. I watch Jericho laugh as he listens, then a tear rolls down his cheek. He wipes it away before the others can see. He knows I am watching him and gives me a toothy grin.

In a quiet moment, as the others are making their way back up to camp, I ask him about his reaction to the news.

'It is my children,' he says.

I shake my head, unable to comprehend.

'The dead have two shadows Gavin, one black that represents the flesh and one white that represents the soul. You saw two of each, it is my children playing.'

He says nothing else, simply turns and walks away, melting into the darkness. Leaving me alone with only confusion for company.

I don't know if it is my illness or my pride that has turned me into a liar, perhaps it is a combination of both. I end the call after speaking to my wife and son; telling them both that I am in good health, and that the doctor who had suggested the trip 'inadvisable' was overreacting. The word he actually used was 'insanity', although I may have left that out under her review. It had taken half an hour after the climb up to make the call, as my breathing was so laboured I thought my chest would literally burst. Luckily, the events of the day had taken the spotlight and attention was detracted from my ailing health. The guys had asked again after my situation, but I had stuck with the flu story. The decision to dive as a four man unit the following day, and not in separate pairs, has convinced me to go ahead. This way everyone is safe and covered by the numbers.

I lie in my tent, thinking about Jericho's words and the seemingly absurd notion that what I saw may in fact have been spirits. I cannot explain what has happened but the rational part of my brain will not let me believe that is the explanation. I don't wonder for long as the weariness in my beleaguered body ushers me into a deep sleep.

Most of the work for the big event was done by the time they rouse me. I do feel better but the climb down takes its toll. Still, the prolonged stint of going through our gear gives me time to recoup. Jericho is, as always, by my side, his excitement infectious. He comes close just as we are preparing to get going.

'In this area it's the custom that when a n'anga dies...' he pauses, his silence asking me if I know who or what that was. I nod him on. 'When a n'anga dies, his possessions are wrapped in a cloth and thrown from the cliffs. Do not touch these things. It will bring back luck.' His tone is solemn and stern in its delivery.

I give a nod of comprehension, and he helps me hoist one of the tanks onto my back.

The time comes and we enter the deep blue for the last time. A prayer is said and we slip below. The journey down is smooth and our close-knit unit sinks ever deeper, equalising our ears as we go. At 85 metres we start pumping air into our BCs to slow our descent. My chest is tight but still I manage to control the urge to cough. Our bottom time is planned for just 12 minutes as our ascent and decompression stops will be a lot longer than the previous dives. The ground appears below us and the torch beams play across the rock surface. The area is not big, and at the far end is another tunnel that extends further down. Its depth has never been determined but its fatality list is testament to its peril.

Jericho was right about the n'anga's possessions: broken pottery, glass and other small trinkets lie among the loose rocks, glinting and reflecting our light. A piece of fabric floats near the cavern wall and hovers like a scarecrow guarding the belongings of the long-since dead.

I press the communication button on my mask. 'There's traditional beliefs surrounding all this stuff, guys. We need to treat it with respect.' In the beam of my torch three thumbs-up come back in reply.

I had held my bearings on the descent, drawing an imaginary line from the top of the rock 108 metres above down to the bottom. I turn in that direction and begin searching the rocks for any signs of the children. Nothing is visible. I move to my left and swish at the silt with my hand; it barely moves. With both hands I creep up the wall until my fins are inches above the floor and kick frantically. Almost instantly, I am enveloped by a cloud of sediment. I slide back down, shining the beam onto the area I have uncovered. My breathing falters and a lump forms in my throat.

Two small skeletons lie next to each other, arms intertwined, on each of their wrists a row of beaded bracelets that sway in the current I have created. I sob at the sight. It comes from a place so deep within me that it hurts as it comes out. I know this will give Jericho the peace he so greatly deserves.

I take the camera from the pouch on my belt, and photograph their final resting place. They look so content. So at ease.

The first bracelet I try to extract snaps immediately, the beads scattering into the silt. I curse my stupidity and try again with gentler hands. Two more break but I manage to save six, which I place in my dive pouch. My actions have drawn my friends to me. They watch in silence, they too humbled by the sight of the remains.

Eventually, Will taps his watch. We have one last swim over the cave floor before beginning our ascent. I recount Jericho's story on the way up. These are good people, worthy people. Worthy enough to hear of the old man's torment. They will respect his pain.

We break surface to the delight of Jack. He whoops and claps at our achievement, and hugs his son close as he gets out of the water. Jericho doesn't move from his spot and, for the first time, avoids eye contact. The guys, although exhausted, do not delay in packing up their gear. They want to give Jericho and me space. Hell, Will even refuses a beer that Jack has brought down, saying, 'We'll have a knuckle-full when we get back to camp.' As each man leaves, he goes over to the old man and pats his shoulder. He looks up at each of them a little bewildered. Not a word is said.

At last I turn to Jericho, summoning him over with a wave of my hand. We sit under an overhang in the shade, and I turn the camera on. The stills of his children's remains fill the screen and I turn it to face him.

'I found them, Jericho. I found your children.'

He blinks, looking deeply at the picture on the screen before him. He takes a bit of time to process the picture but, when he gets it, the tears roll freely down his cheeks. I dig in my dive pouch and lightly extract the bracelets. His eyes shine, and the tears of sadness seem to be overrun by tears of joy. He gingerly takes his treasure and presses it against his cheek. That's the spot I leave him in, holding his past in the palm of his hands.

I have demons of my own to slay. I need to come clean with my friends and family, I need their forgiveness and support. Then, perhaps, I too can find closure. Find peace.

Missed Call

Murenga Joseph Chikowero

My big sister, Sisi Dudu, never left Zimbabwe. No, not even when the teapot-shaped country heated and hissed to a searing boil as the economy staggered and stumbled but finally made up its mind to just limp along like a sick old man who stubbornly clings to life until those gathered to witness his passing give up and return to their own homes, scratching their heads and muttering darkly. 'I love sadza nenyama cooked on firewood,' Sisi Dudu told Mother. I had not spoken to her in years now but we used Mother as the conveyor of messages about each other. I do not know exactly when I made the decision to stop directly communicating with her but it could have been in my second year in college. I had grown weary of this Dudu, the smallness of her life. She wrote of a life dominated by a stern mother-in-law who sniffed around her all day. I chose to cling to the memory of Dudu, the schoolgirl whose dreams seemed too beautiful to be crushed by a thing as ordinary as a marriage. So I kept, read and re-read her old letters, revisited text messages about her from Mother. Sometimes Mother shared entire conversations the two of them had had.

I knew about Sisi Dudu's two kids and she knew I had left. She had written long letters that described the details of the people in her life and drew only the faintest outlines of her own life. I read and reread the letters that I had received years ago, looking for clues in the full, rounded characters that sat on the lines. I had known her long enough to know her real feelings were revealed by what she said about other people, not herself. And so I scoured the parts about her children, who were everything to her. Dudu was, after all, notorious for telling a story and then just leaving it there like a shirt pocket that clings to a shirt by a

148

thread. I read each of these letters and examined the occasional picture that she enclosed, hunting for clues about this sister of mine whose dreams had been shattered by a marriage to a bus conductor.

I was not angry with Dudu when she dropped her dreams like a hot earthen pot and married. She had seemed detached from the marriage rituals. I was angry at our once shared dreams, which now lay in the dust like a weather-beaten shoe from bygone years. She had married, my Sisi Dudu, a man who was to go missing one stormy night not too long after the marriage. It was as if my sister had been running up the brown gravel path to the school like every other sixteen-year-old one day and somehow married the next. It felt like an unfunny joke, the whole thing, like a man who excuses himself halfway into a game of mini-soccer and leaves the country altogether. It was Dudu who had taught me about big universities out there and we were supposed to attend one of them one day.

I disliked him on sight, the too-cheerful mouse of a man who married Dudu. I had only been vaguely aware of him until he showed up at our home. He was a conductor for one of the few public buses that still ran the Ngezi-Harare route. He brought his uncle to negotiate roora the day after our headmaster reminded us the examination fees were due in a week's time. I had overheard enough of my parents' conversations to know Dudu was not going to be around much longer. And that perhaps part of her roora was going to end up as my examination fees. I felt sick and considered quitting school for a while.

'Ah, tsano, sit here and tell me how school is treating you,' my soon-to-be brother-in-law smiled widely as if he meant for me to count his teeth. 'School is OK,' keen to prove that his charm was not working.

I looked at Dudu as she busied herself at the hearth, head cast to one side. This man was seeing a wife, but I was seeing my only sibling in the world, Dudu the maths genius, Dudu the fun-loving sister who had taught me fish-fish-spell-your-name as we skipped rope, her feet beating a gentle rhythm in the dust. I was seeing Dudu the big sister who had one day picked up an empty Willards Potato Chips packet and taught me Zsa Zsa the Scarlet, Mama Chompkin, Putzi the Dog, Professor Flubb, Jake the Pirate, Harry the Hip. It seemed like just the other day when Dudu and I had caught butterflies and rubbed colour off their wings on to our bodies as we uttered what fancy clothes we would wear in the future.

'I will wear a nice blue hat,' she would say as she rubbed a butterfly's wings on her hair.

'I will wear nice brown shoes,' I would join in, rubbing away at my dusty feet. Together we had painted our shared futures of blue hats, shiny brown shoes, and grand universities.

And now, all these adults were going to gather and agree that Dudu could be married off just like that! As if Dudu and I had not shared dreams of travelling the world and learning at famous universities out there. Makerere was her favourite, simply because she loved how the name tasted on her tongue. It seemed as if one minute Dudu's maths teacher was speaking highly of her talent with numbers on prize-giving day and the next she was packing her clothes, including her school uniform, into one of Mother's changani travel bags to begin an uncertain life among strange people.

A week after our extended family had gathered to receive roora, Dudu woke up in the morning, wordlessly made tea for all of us as usual, took a bath in the grass bathroom outside and put on one of her better dresses. She slipped into the girls' room and emerged with her changani bag, a faraway look in her eye. I looked up at her face but she would not meet my gaze.

'The bus to Njanja leaves Chivhu at two o'clock. I must be at 52 Miles by at least midday because the buses to Masvingo are usually full,' she said to no one in particular, turning her left arm inwards to check her new watch, the one her husband had brought her on his most recent visit before the roora ceremony proper. She was repeating the bus schedules between our village in Ngezi, 52 Miles on the Harare to Masvingo highway, the little town of Chivhu towards Masvingo and this unknown new home of hers called Njanja, where people apparently gave birth to boys who grew up to look like this man.

He had brought gifts for everyone, this man who was marrying my sister. Mother got a roll of colourful cloth for dresses while Father got a cap, a necktie too bright for his age, a pair of steel-toed shoes that broke the earth as he walked and enough snuff to satisfy ten giants. And Father was not even a giant. I got a thin roll of twenty-dollar notes all to myself, the green ones with an image of the elephant and Mosi-oa-Tunya. They were old notes that had passed though the hands and pockets of many unknown users in their time. I flipped and examined each of them, ignoring Father's obvious embarrassment. But I was not done just yet. I held each by its corners with both hands and held it to the light to check for kasimbi kegoridhe, the thin metallic strip in the middle that we were told was made of pure gold and proved a bill was genuine.

That is how my sister went to her husband's family in Njanja, bearing two children by the time I had sleepwalked through my undergraduate classes and chose to do odd holiday jobs rather than visit the village.

'Your mukuwasha is buying his own kombi,' my sister wrote in one letter. It was always 'your mukuwasha' and never 'my husband'.

I looked at the pictures of the man in question. He seemed to have become just another bored-looking man who now let his beard grow any way it wanted. Gone was the too-wide smile on his face or maybe he just stopped smiling for photographs. My sister stood there in the photograph, right next to the unsmiling man. They stood close as if at the request of the photographer, only their shoulders touching, staring into the soul of the camera. I was relieved to note the children took after their mother even as they assumed their father's stiff pose. There was no mention of any more dollar bills for me, I noted. I was glad to hear from Dudu, to know she was still out there, that perhaps she still nursed a dream even in what I thought of as her bleak existence. Not too long after that, I found it harder and harder to write back, at first taking weeks to summon the energy to write and then stopping altogether. Mother will tell her how I am doing anyway, I found what I thought was a plausible excuse.

I was not saddened when word reached me that the bearded one, my sister's husband, had died or, more precisely, disappeared. Mother and Father went to Njanja to commiserate with their son-in-law's family, but I avoided the event entirely, making a vague excuse in a letter. Apparently the bearded one's driver had attempted to cross a flooded Munyati River bridge one night and the bus was swept away by the current. Everybody on the bus was shaken but accounted for, all, that is, except Daddy Longbeard. One theory was that a mermaid living in the quiet, bottomless pool down the river had abducted him and made him a husband, but I was sceptical. What kind of mermaid wants Mr Ugly Beard for a husband? My own unspoken theory was that the schoolgirl-snatching bastard had seized the moment of chaos at the bridge to take off with the little bag containing the day's takings since he was still a bus conductor. You never know with men who don't care to manage their own beard, I concluded maliciously.

When I finished my degree programme at university, I worked only briefly in Harare, then gathered my things and took off. Young people with any kind of qualification were already looking far and wide. Britain was an attractive destination for many because almost everyone knew someone who was already there. But I wanted to go so far I would not hear even the echoes of my footfalls. That is how I applied to a programme in development studies at a university in an American state whose name I had never heard spoken before. As if the snow and strange accent that made every sentence sound like a question were not bad enough, every other class I took attacked me with images of children carrying AK47 rifles, children carrying ammunition belts and other children running away from battle scenes. It was the image of a teary child pulling at his dying mother in one textbook that stopped me cold.

I told my advisor I needed a week to sort out urgent family affairs and she grudgingly agreed. I took to wearing dark glasses everywhere and visiting the thrift store where I spent hours examining donated books, clothes, shoes, radios and music on tape, CD and vinyl. I tried to imagine what story lay behind each ancient radio or vinyl, things obviously dumped by families whose great aunt or grandmother had passed on and nobody knew what to do with them. The books often gave some clues; many of them gifts from aunties to nephews, happy birthdays and merry Christmases wished in slow, careful cursive. I was busy delving into one of these books, a pictorial volume on *The Bantus of Africa*, when my phone buzzed in my left shirt pocket, like a gentle tap tap tap to the heart underneath. 'Sisi Dudu calling', my phone informed me. I had asked for her number from Mother as soon as I heard she had bought a cell phone but had adamantly refused to make the first move by calling her. I guess I had become used to hearing about her rather than actually talking to her.

I thought about dashing to my car in the parking lot but knew it would be cold after sitting there for a while. I retreated to an adjoining room almost at a trot, making throaty noises to remind Sisi Dudu that I was still on the line. I must talk to her from some quiet corner. Why exactly had I been angry with Sisi Dudu, my only sibling in the entire world, I wondered as I looked for a quiet corner. No door separated the two warehouse-style rooms but this second room carried no clothing items at all. Rather, it was bursting with all manner of electronic equipment: radios bearing brand names that were either no longer in existence or had changed names; WRS, RCA, SUPERSONIC, TRIDENT; and stacks upon stacks of vinyl records, what my uncle, a collector, used to call long plays.

'Hello Sisi Dudu,' I began, unsure how to begin.

But the phone was dead.

Missed.

My mouth remained open, still mouthing Sisi Dudu's name.

Moaning about these false missed calls from home was a pet gripe among all African students. Such calls showed up as missed calls on the phone screen but it was known that the caller knew what they were doing; they ended the call after two or three buzzes, roughly the time it took to fish the phone from the pocket but not enough time for the receiver to actually answer it. But I felt no such unhappiness now. I zipped past the counter where the clerk was weighing a customer's used clothes and trotted to my beat-up car at the back of the store. The engine responded at the third try. Rain had replaced the snow of the past season. Buds were already appearing at the end of tree branches. A robin or two even tweeted the beginning of Spring. I drove past the university campus on the hill and found the Mexican-owned store where they sold airtime.

'Give me two ten-dollar cards, please,' I said, sliding over a twenty-dollar bill. I drove to my rathole of a studio apartment and waited for nightfall in Zimbabwe, when cell phone charges were lowest.

The Sea

Gamu Chamisa

You walk into the house. Work has been hard, and Melbourne's petulant heat leaves a film of sweat on top of your careful makeup. It is muggy out so your blouse stays damp in patches, and you are sticky, restless. The summer lords furious, irrepressible, through into March and sends you to the beach at night on breathless little trips to the water and to new air, to where the sea and sky touch and quiet mind, to some kind of calm that stills your heart to soft.

You leave your work clothes on the bathroom floor and stand under the spray of the shower. The water is cool and you wash the smell of coconut into your skin and then rub the velvet of whipped shea butter into your new stretch marks, try to dull the edge of this new ugly etched indelible into your skin.

Ray comes home to you tired, with dirt under his fingernails and grease smeared on the seat of his pants. His hair, a triumphant shout of young dreadlocks, is unruly as always, and you feel the familiar prickle of annoyance at his puerile unkemptness. He smells strongly of cigarettes and vaguely of sweat and that woody cologne you bought him last Christmas.

You don't know how this happened. You realise this, with a sigh, with a sagging of shoulders, with that sinking feeling. You don't know how this happened.

Ray is too tall for you. His teeth are misarranged almost comically, awful, and his heart is sometimes hard, sometimes inconstant, but. The but that has kept you here. Goddamn. In the right light, in the soft moments, there is *something* about him. And so here you are. Couldn't explain it if you tried. Two almost-adults playing at family, fumbling into a future. You look at this tower of man, and he reminds you of places he has never even seen, places where you grew up, you and Leo. Leo, your moon, your brother who hasn't spoken to you in years. Ray reminds you of wishes you made when you were younger: wishing for the water to work, wishing for life and its ordinariness and its daily routine because all around you was a tumult and the extraordinary heartbreak of watching your mother die. Now the bedlam is in you, and all around is life, a life, *your* life, quietly unfolding itself neatly in gentle squares. Your body is here, your life is here in tax forms and spent days and passport stamps and your signature on the bottom line. And Ray is here. Ray, who is almost like Harare and Dakar, a pulsing memory of all the winterless years of your childhood, in that he nearly feels like home. Nearly.

Now.

You are almost certain that the baby will have Ray's smile. Braces will be a necessity. You are also sure that your child will have the softness that settles in his eyes when he is quiet and sleepy and watching television with you, his limbs draped over yours because he is vulnerable and tender with that grating casualness of his. Haphazardly lovely, carelessly open. Tender, his body weaving with yours because those are things that lovers do. Lazy Sundays, long Friday nights, pasta for dinner on Wednesdays. A routine of just being there, just being together. Dreamy, his head against your chest, kink grazing your jaw, his open palm pressed gently against the swell of your belly. Your perfectly rehearsed sighs nesting in his hair. Softness shared. When he speaks, you can hear the wonder in his voice, the awe, the gratitude. You don't say much, you have plenty to say but you just don't know how to begin. You are quiet, you carry silence in your middle. A lot on your mind, you just don't know how to begin, tongue-tied, head full to the brim of sad things swirling.

You want to tell him.

You can't sleep at night. It's not the heat or the aches or inevitable discomforts of pregnancy, it's not the baby playing his games in your belly or pushing up into your ribs, it is the lie. Pretending not to be afraid is draining and tiresome and cruel to yourself. Holding parts of yourself in, away from his view, has become too much.

You want to pull down your walls. You want to tell Ray, the sky, the sea, your baby-self, you want to tell Leo.

Love is your father holding and soothing your mother as she trembled and shrunk, her vomit slick and foul in his lap. It is the acid in his voice as he barks at you to leave the room. You stumble out, that image imprinted forever in your head, something no child should ever see. Later on your father orders you out of hospital rooms, tells Leo to hold your hand in the passageway before the doctors give him and Mummy the news, so you don't hear the words that finally broke their hope – *inoperable, metastasised, palliate* – so you don't see your parents cling to each other and cry. Leo, disobeying, Leo, firstborn and responsible, sneaks into the shared room and stands on a chair behind a curtain and hears everything. Love is loss, is big, is terror, is devastating, is big brother never crying, is whispers and denial and standing outside closed doors waiting to get let in.

This now, this here, is something smaller, something stickier. It is immaturity and mistakes, mistrust and a yellow kind of desperation, it is you afraid of raising a child on your own because you are not strong like your father, and a fear of being alone finally (you are always lonely), and it is Ray holding on too tightly in endless apology. It is two kinds of selfish settled to cohabit one skin, feeding off each other. You tell yourself it is love, and that lie haunts you because you have seen it real, you have known it.

Love is Harare buzzing vibrant in December. It is in a wedding photograph from Dakar in the eighties, and a photo of three, two adults and one little Leo, in stonewashed jeans and white shirts before Yaya was born and the three became four. It is a home full of grace and soft accents and all the wonderful smells of your mama's cooking. It was your mother's patience and warmth even when she was tired and sick (before you could properly tell she was ill, before her skin lost its glow and her bones lost their flesh, and her head lost its hair). Love was her patience with teaching you your languages so you know her laughter and her whispers and her songs in four tongues. Her unselfconsciousness with her Shona that was always worse than yours, less natural, seasoned with mishandled syllables and verbs, is a beautiful memory.

'Language is political,' she said once to your father. You were maybe six or seven years old. This was after you had shown them the circular from the headmistress at the junior school, the letter urging parents of *local* grade one and two students to speak to their children exclusively in English at home. For the time being. There was a list of recommended daytime viewing and bedtime reading (Enid Blyton and the like) attached. So as to encourage the children's transition into the anglophone education system, improve their accents, expand their vocabularies. Et cetera. Less chiShona, less isiNdebele, more English, untwist the black babies' tongues and iron out the creases of culture.

'Language is political,' Mama repeated to you as if you could have understood. Then she gestured for you to sit at her feet so she could neaten your mabhanzi. Reluctantly you obeyed, and braced yourself because while Mama's voice was gentle her hands were not. She continued. 'Language connects you, and Leo, and me, and Baba, and all of our grandmothers and grandfathers. It connects us with our histories, Yao. Always be proud of your words. Do you hear me, Leo? Your brother, always buried in his books, don't just read them, write, *speak*. Don't lose your words.'

'Your mother is right,' your father said, full of adoration. Or perhaps matter-of-factly. The memories are polished to a glow that can't always be true. But, who cares really, your memories are *yours*. Pictures and memories are all you have, and the years keep rolling on, pulling you further from that six-year-old and her mama. You grieve through remembering and you want to believe that in every moment they were together, from when they met that year in Paris – Mama was studying and Baba was working for that bank – until the end, you want to believe that Baba adored her. Your mother was a woman who deserved to be adored. That particular evening, when you were six and Leo was ten and Mama wasn't sick yet, Baba smiled and said, 'Your mother is right.' He ripped the letter from St. Catherine's in two and smiled at your mother. 'She's always right,' he laughed, and she laughed, and she relented her grip on your edges, and the whole room felt warm and safe, and you knew then, even as a child, that this is love, this is the beautiful face of love.

Love was your father holding your and Leo's hands, saying everything would be alright when the withered, exhausted version of your mother finally drifted off, drunk off pain meds, breath fading from the morphine and the organ failure. Dad had kisses for you, and gentleness despite his own grief. With Leo he had arguments, moody teenaged Leo whose grief was fierce, whose anger was immense. With you he was Leo still, just a little frayed, but he was still big brother who looked out for you and taught you little mischiefs and shared secrets and silences. He was still himself, and your father was still himself. So the beast between them, that ferocity of Leo's contempt, didn't make sense. You didn't understand why Leo pushed your father away, your father who held you tightly until you fell asleep every night for weeks, your father who learnt from Sisi Joyce – with initially much awkwardness and mirth – how to thread your hair into mabhanzi, your father who paid for a French tutor, who sent you to your mother's family when he could afford it, so you wouldn't forget.

You didn't understand when Leo shouted, 'You bastard! You could have saved her, you let her go.'

You didn't understand then, and neither did Leo, you suspect, and how could he, he was fourteen, neither of you could have understood then the costs of living, of dying, of being sick in a country with broken PET scan machines in its graveyard hospitals and striking nurses and doctors and a scarcity of specialists and medicines.

Leo was angry. Leo is proud.

You haven't spoken in five years. You think about him every day. He hasn't seen your father since he left for university. It's been eight years. Leo broke your father's heart, Leo abandoned you.

The last thing he said to you, bitterly, 'I'm sorry you feel that way. You were a child, there is so much you didn't see or hear. There are a lot of things you wouldn't have understood. He made her give up so much for him, her career, her family, for what? His job working at a bank that exploits and steals? He didn't love her enough.'

But how could he not have loved her? You know now about dying with some kind of dignity. Mama died in her own bed with her babies close and her songs soft in the room. How could he never have loved her?

You have the memories of love, but you use the name in vain now and so cast a spell that takes the sleep from your nights and the peace from your bones and the words from your mouth. You panic. The water is rising up to your throat. Loss feels inevitable and you are tired of being vigilant against it. Mama was sick, you could not help that, but you failed to save your brother and your father, you tried to talk them down, you tried to be there, to help, but you did not do enough. Little daughter, little sister, no might in your fists, too little conviction in your voice.

'Leo, I swear to God if you leave me, Leo, I swear to God if you leave us—'

'You swear what? Yaya, what? How are you going to punish me? What are you and Dad going to do? There's nothing you can take away from me, there's nothing for me here or in SA. I want to leave. Fuck this house, fuck Dad, fuck this country.'

'Leo, please. I need you. Stay, you are all I have.' You were fourteen, he was pushing nineteen.

'I'm sorry, Yaya. I want to live, I want to leave.'

You feel Leo in the roots of your hair, sometimes, in the arch of your foot, sometimes. Elemental. Sometimes. He is mute and rage – ebbing, ebbing, and then crash – and gorgeous, and dreamy. You see his face as a teenager, Leo, half-man, half-boy, with your father's nose spread on his face.

You want to tell him, you were there too. You lost too. Mama wouldn't want this, her family a shambles. You want to tell him you remember.

When you were younger – Leo was fourteen, you were ten –your maman and your baba took you to France on holiday. To visit Mama's brothers. Baba and Mama took you to Euro Disneyland and to the Eiffel Tower, and, better than it all, they took you to the water.

Your mother was so beautiful, and it's a shame you don't really look like her. Too much of your father in you. She is so beautiful in all the photographs and old videos, her skin is flawless ebony, and even in the stills you can tell her laugh is big and her skin smells like home. It echoes still, through your mind, through your bones. Mama was lovelier translated to her French that summer, that June, whereas your father's English-Shona tongue, which fumbled, heavy, with the twang of vowels and caught on the curves of cédilles, was inelegant. Everybody laughed, and your father joined in, was expansive and indulgent. He watched football and talked economic policy with Uncle P, and in the kitchen you and Leo stayed close to your mother and the aunties. Leo was watchful, a sentinel, his eyes hungry. You got in the way and you memorised the shape of Mama's legs while you looked up at her from a tangle on the floor. You memorised the feel of her hands on your face, you somehow knew not to take it for granted. That summer.

There is healing in the water, Mama told you on the flight to her brothers. *And I want you kids to spend some time with my side of the family. So you don't forget them.*

It didn't work, the water, the visit to her family, the prayer, the doctors, it didn't work. None of it. Eight months later Mama was gone.

'Yaya.' His voice comes to you now, climbs up the ledge and pulls you away from the places you want to explore, to fall into and drown in. Ray.

'Hey...' you say, a little tired, a little wary.

'Come to bed.' Ray speaks with a soft smile and shining eyes. He is all of your demons, with a soft smile and shining eyes. He is your future, and you know it already, you know already that you are settling. You are relinquishing something, you are becoming old. You want to run, you want to jump, but here he is, pulling you back to enfold you in your quiet terror. Into the limits of an Us. Your mother is not here to teach you the lessons, she is not here to give you the courage to act decisively instead of just going along with the flow of a life, of this life, of *your* life now. Mama isn't here to stroke your cheek, or rub your back while you weep, and soothe, *Oh Yao, oh Yao, look at the mess you've made. We'll fix it.*

'Yaya... come to bed.'

Ray lies beneath you, breathless. Your bodies tangle and rise and move and stretch. You shout at his eyelashes, at his fingertips, you tear at his arms. You wrap yourself in him like a dream, but you can't get close enough, he arches over everything like a sky, but you can't escape thoughts of your brother and your father, of your mother, of the silence growing inside of you. You cannot forget, you cannot forget, *Oh Yao, oh... Yaya.*

'You have a sweet nature, like your mama, but you also have her fire,' Uncle P told you, looking into you, seeing you. You were ten, Leo was fourteen. Uncle P touched your hair which was long and thick and healthy, unlike Mama's since she had (suddenly and randomly, you thought at the time) cropped it short and had taken to wearing multicoloured doeks, and headwraps that seemed to sing, 'vraiment, just like her.' You looked up at your uncle, you saw his sad eyes and you held your breath. You don't look like your mother, and it's a pity, but maybe somewhere in you you have her heart.

The uncles sat down in the late afternoon sunshine and played their old records, and your mother and Tante Lou-lou sang the songs from their adolescence. The cousins (you haven't seen them since) danced and clapped. You and Leo stole a bottle of beer from the kitchen and shared it in tumblers (Uncle P noticed but said nothing, conspiring in your fun with an indulgent smile), and you got silly and sweet and open. You saw, not for the first time, the way your father looked at your mother – he had the night in his eyes, and his night-eyes were full of stars and oceans. Ray does not look at you like that, and that is something you have always known. He comes home to you, and brings you flowers sometimes, and holds you close when you tell him you're pregnant and maybe you're keeping it and breathes a heavy 'okay' into your neck – he is a tower – but he does not look at you with an entire sky aglow in his eyes.

You like the beach, now, always, you like the seaside and the feel of the sun on your skin and the sound of the water crashing into itself and being pulled in and sent back in endless games by the shore. You see Mama in her loose maxi dresses getting her feet and hemline wet and giggling with Leo. You recall the safety in Baba's arms as he swept you up (even though you were big and long-limbed for ten) and rushed you into the dancing water. You luxuriate in the infinity of the blue-green touching the pale-bright horizon. You revel in the thought of how deep the water is, you torture yourself with the delicious idea, the immense temptation, of drifting and drowning – salt water down your throat, salt water to fill your lungs – and letting the sea take your body. Elemental. Looking for the healing. It makes your gums ache and your bones warm. Since you were a child. You are happiest by the water, calmest, most certain of peace, unafraid of death, warm to the idea of it. Since you were a child. Sure. There may not be healing in the water, but there is an aloneness that makes sense, an insignificance, body versus ocean, that is so beautiful it hurts, that gives perspective and scale, however ephemeral. The sea is so beautiful as you stand and watch it, shimmer on the surface dancing, and it calls your name. The same sea it appears to you – sudden, calm, devastating, *home* – in Dromana with Ray or with a blur of friends at Portarlington, or at Sandy Bay over that lonely Christmas holiday with Dad just over a year ago, or in Marseille as a child, or in Saly before then, it looks the same, it is the same. Always the incomparable sense of it, the roar and echo, the size of it, the sea, always the endlessness. It calls out and you answer in a voice that is not your own.

Oh yes, you moan. *Yes,* always. Always, *yes.*

Your father calls every other day with news of home, of his life where he is, demanding attention, demanding your voice, your laugh, your breath. He calls to talk about you and Ray and he swears he is not disappointed in you. He's excited for a grandchild. He never talks about Leo, or the new woman Tete Grace says he is *seeing with intention,* doesn't answer questions about her or the possibility of giving you step-siblings, so you can't ask him if Mama was not enough. He calls to ask if you have had your screening yet, and he shouts when the answer is no. He shouts and then apologises, he says he understands your fear, and you can feel his heavy hug from across the distance, his shoulders sagging and his arms heavy, through the depth of the things that separate father and daughter. You can feel his worry, and to your shame you savour it. Cruelty comes too easily in your muted world.

The sight of your dying mother splintered something inside of you. And inside of fourteen-year-old Leo too, you learnt later. She was thirty-six. It was sad. You cried, loud, lost in the performance of fear, screaming, at the funeral. Leo didn't. Her voice, her touch, her skin and bones were gone forever, and you didn't understand the hugeness of it in that moment, you couldn't fathom the permanence of a grave or a tombstone or that wordless goodbye, of the silence that follows. You couldn't understand until you looked out at the horizon from the beach. Forever. Always. Eternity. You miss your mama, you miss your Leo. You miss being whole and living out loud.

The symmetry of it, a stab to the heart. A bad joke. God is laughing. Your mother was twenty-two when she had your brother, and you stand, sand between your toes, now, at that same age, twenty-two years old with a baby blooming in you. A son. Emmanuel for your mother, Emmanuelle.

You listen to the waves now. The sun stings your bare shoulders. You place your hands on your belly, your almost fully-grown bump of baby. You sigh. Will he look like Ray? Will you wrap this child in your threadbare French and moth-eaten Wolof, and kiss his tiny feet while he sleeps? Emmanuel. Leo doesn't know about him yet. Your heart hurts. Is your blood feeding baby with disease and despair? You sigh and the sea asks again in soft tones... You answer. *Yes*. Always, *yes*.

Oh but you can't leave your father, he cannot lose everyone, it's not fair, it's not right. But still... your answer is yes as you watch the end of the world glinting so beautiful, stunning, stunning, the diamonds on the water. You feel your mother in your bones. And Leo. The water is cool, delightful against your ankles, then your knees, it rises, getting colder, it laps against your belly. It is glorious. You shiver, can't quite seem to catch your breath, you are sobbing, your chest burns tight, and tears slip down your face. Salt to salt. *Toujours*. Yes. Always, yes.

The wind picks up, snatches away Ray's frantic shouts from the shore. The water pulls at your drenched clothes, and you walk deeper still. Everything is loud, the world has colour now.

The memory comes again, comes again. Leo was fourteen, you were ten, on the sunny perfect azure coast. Before your mother's sickness claimed her, before your father's heart broke, before your brother grew into an anger he cannot come back from. That summer resonates infinite. He took your hand, Leo. He knew already, he had seen, he had heard. Half-boy, half-man, he was trying to do something about it.

'Hold my hand, Yaya. There is healing in the water. We'll find it for her.' You took his hand, you held it tightly. You had your brother then, now you are alone in the world. You looked up at him and he was smiling. He led you. 'Come, Yaya.'

Mama called out to you, but the horizon called louder. And Leo led you. Leo, a safety.

Yaoundé! The shore screamed. Now, Ray in a panic and running into the shallows.

Yaya... The ocean sang, siren. Sleepwalking, day-falling, sky-dreaming, knees fizzing, heart adrift.

Always yes. *Yes.*

You held onto your brother's hand and walked into the sea.

These Feet Were Made for Walking

Blessing Musariri

In all his eighty-four good but often trying years on earth, Papa Sikala had never witnessed anything as disturbing as the events that took place at the funeral of his old friend Baptista Muvengi. Chikare village was in such a state of high excitement that Papa Sikala, often reluctant to join in any public arousal, quite forgot himself and succumbed to the prevailing sentiment. He had never put so much as a pair of plastic slippers on his feet, yet here he was counting out his last few dollars for his grandson Taku to buy him a pair of slippers and a bag of coarse salt.

'Kule, you are too old to be afraid of witches, what would they want with you? They can't use you to do anything – how far would you go?' Taku stood impatiently on the riskier side of the threshold, wearing his perfectly off-white pair of almost new tennis shoes, with green and pink detailing. It was a rare occasion for his feet to find their way into the slightly tight canvas caverns but, with his only pair of patapatas having breathed their last two days before, Taku had no choice. He wiggled his toes experimentally and tried to accustom himself to the suffocation of his feet.

'Heeee! Taku, you are young and stupid, what do you know? I do more work in a day than you do in a week, now go before I take your shoes and go to plant maize in them. Only good thing your father ever did – his head was just as empty as yours.'

'Crazy old man!' Taku muttered as he walked away from the homestead.

Standing in the cool eaves of his thatched roof, Papa Sikala indulged in some muttering of his own. '... empty as a bottle, only you can fill a

165

bottle with water, what of empty heads? Aaaiiiiii ya ya!' With a great big sigh, he turned away from the door to sit down on the low stoep running along the entire wall of the circular hut. His grandson Taku was a blessing, albeit one in a very good disguise. Sometimes he was quite simply a burden.

'I know how far the shop is,' he called out even though he knew he was talking to himself, 'don't be gone all day!' As he spoke the last word, Papa Sikala wondered why he even bothered to waste his breath, precious as it was lately.

Indeed Papa Sikala had reason to worry about letting Taku out of his sight. There was yet a day Taku had completed his walk to the centre without bumping into the nemesis that insisted on calling himself a friend. Jameson was good fun only if you didn't allow his coercive demon into any minute of your day, only if you did not depend on him and only if you parted ways almost as soon as you met.

'Taku! Hey Taku mfana! Wait up!' Jameson jogged up from somewhere in the long grass. It seemed to Taku that he had conjured himself from thin air – almost as if he was some lost spirit condemned to haunt that stretch of road, only to be allowed beyond it in the company of those unsuspecting.

'Ey Jam'son! I'm not mfana wako and I don't have time to hang about with you. Kule has sent me to buy slippers and salt and they have nothing left at the shop so I have to go kugrowth point and that will take me longer. The old man was already complaining before I left. I want him to kill his old rooster for supper tonight so I have to keep him happy.'

'Forget about your stomach for once. So it's true? Tell me if it's true.' Jameson's lean frame towered over Taku's, shorter and sturdier. Taku walked on, resolute, but he failed to resist the seduction of having been at the scene of such a scintillating tale. It simply had to be told.

'Wena! You know this mfana waSoni, what's his name again? Can't recall! But yah, him, came to the funeral, greeted everyone and then walked to the casket during the body viewing. People thought he was leaning down to kiss the body, which was strange enough, but iwe! He bit off the nose! You should have seen him. He fought off grown men like mad Mzana when the bee stung him in the groin.' Jameson folded over laughing until Taku, giving in, also gasped with laughter.

'Shaz, I'm laughing now but it wasn't funny! It can only be bewitchment. Can you imagine biting the nose off a corpse – Mudhara Muvengi for that matter, whose nose was always full of snot and snuff? Thoo!' Taku spat into the grass. 'I've always known there were witches but this is going too far, Jam'son. We can't just sit and let some witch put spells on us to do their work in broad daylight. That's why I'm on my way to buy slippers for Kule, and coarse salt to sprinkle around our place so the witches don't come near. Everyone is doing this, it's the only way.'

'Haaahhhh! Forget about that, man. Any witch would be cursed to have you as an errand boy, you are lazy and you don't follow instructions.' Again, Jameson folded over in laughter. Taku, annoyed, picked up his pace and walked with determination.

'Iwe mhani! Leave me alone.' He shrugged off Jameson's placating hand on his shoulder.

'Ah come on muface wangu. Let's see who will finally give us our first taste of beer. What does the old man need shoes for now? If anyone was going to bewitch him they would have done so a long time ago. Anyway he's going to die soon, so why waste money?'

'Manje so, Jam'son! Don't talk like that about my grandfather!' It was one thing for Taku to call his grandfather a crazy old man but Jameson often went too far and it was at this precise point in time when one had to employ all resources in parting ways with him.

'Sori, Sori boss!' Jameson was suitably apologetic. 'Your grandfather is my grandfather. But he can wait an hour or so. See, there's the beerhall a few steps away. Mukoma Willie promised me a sip of his scud, I'll ask him to let you have some too.' Taku heard music blaring from a battered speaker, a kombi conductor attempting to harvest passengers from passersby and the faint thrumming sound of the mill. He stopped and faced Jameson with determination.

'Jam'son, I must find these slippers and go back, this is serious business. Kule is stuck inside until I bring him the slippers. I'll come back and join you, it's still early,' he reasoned.

'Ende Taku, you are sooooo boring! What's wrong with you? You're the one who's bewitched, always running back home to Kule.'

'Jam'son, I'm going to hit you just now. Watch it!' Taku warned.

'What? A girl like you!'

It was inevitable. Taku was taken in and the mock fight that ensued culminated in almost uncontrollable bouts of laughter.

'Ha iwe mhani! Come on, just this one time.'

*

Peering into the gloaming, Papa Sikala overpowered the chirping of the crickets with the loud kissing of his teeth.

'Hey wena! Blarry stupid boy. Up to now?' His frail body trembled with the strength of his ire. By the glow of his cooking fire he shuffled back into the hut and rearranged pots and plates on the wooden cabinet with such an unacceptable level of force that the precariously perched lid of a teapot went leaping into the fire. At this, Papa Sikala stopped only long enough to kiss his teeth again and continued pushing his meagre belongings around.

'How does he think I will go to the toilet?'

Finding what he was looking for, the sudden silence was interrupted by the trickle of liquid entering an empty vessel followed by a long sigh of relief.

'Empty bottles are at least good for something, what of empty heads?'

*

At Chakare growth point police lock-up, Taku was engaged in some feisty banging of his own – against the wooden door that had been unceremoniously shut in his face. A slat opened and a pair of disinterested eyes peered into the gloom.

'Please officer. It wasn't my fault. I was just protecting myself and I didn't steal anything, it was–'

The slat closed on his pleading and Taku heard the jingling of keys grow fainter. He shouted louder, even as a sinking feeling invaded his gut.

'Please officer. My grandfather is all alone and he's waiting for his shoes and the salt. If he walks outside without shoes witches will take his footprints and put a spell on him. It's important I have to get home, don't you know...' Taku indulged in more fruitless banging.

'Officer!'

'Officer... please.'

He pressed his ear to the door in the hope of catching the earliest sound of returning footsteps, but they continued to grow fainter and fainter until all he could hear was an uncomfortable ringing in his ear.

'Please send someone to...' He couldn't even bring himself to shout again, but he tried once more, all the while knowing that he was now definitely talking to himself, '... my grandfather.' In the distance, a door banged shut.

Dejected, Taku stared at what he now guessed was the door. If he turned around he wouldn't know which side was which.

'Ey!' he exclaimed to himself, then, 'there's no light in here.' He began again with renewed vigour, 'Officer! Officer!'

The silence that answered his calls was absolute, broken only by the sound of his body sliding resignedly against the wall. A long sigh followed and, slowly, the faint tinkling of music and voices filtered in. Taku took no comfort in this.

'For sure, I'm stupid and Jam'son is a brarry shit!' he muttered.

'Stupid brarry shit!' he shouted, kicking the door, then returned to muttering to himself, 'Stealing people's beer and leaving me to pay for his crime. I should never have listened to him. Wait until I see him. Just wait.'

Taku was startled out of his fit of pique by a sound that was suspiciously like that of a runny nose attempting to reclaim its contents and then, a cough. Drawing his legs in and pushing himself against the door Taku called out cautiously, 'Hey! Who is that?'

His inquiry was met by a sly shuffling, followed by a silence that prickled his skin as if it had become an ephemeral being brushing up against him.

'I said who's there?' he called out louder than before and with more aggression. He was ready to fight. In fact, he would love to hit someone very hard right now and, if it couldn't be Jameson, then any sorry bugger would do. A small voice spoke into the echo of Taku's menace.

'It's me.'

'Me who?'

'Bright.'

'Bright who?'

169

'Madzimure.'

'What are you doing here?'

'Waiting.'

'For what?'

'For the police from Dombo town to come and fetch me.' The small voice was now tearful and Taku relaxed, at least he wasn't alone and it was someone even more distraught than him.

'The officer said they can only come tomorrow.'

'You're just a boy; what have you been arrested for?'

'I don't know. When I woke up I found myself in here.'

'They arrested you while you were sleeping?' Taku was incredulous at the story he was hearing, surely this was a tall tale in the making. People in Chikare were well known for their propensity for embellishment.

'I don't know.' The story was threatening to be more confusing than interesting and Taku stretched out his legs and settled in for the unravelling of it, boring or not, he had nothing better to do anyway, so two plus two could equal nine for all he cared. He decided a little prodding was in order.

'Ey! Mupfana iwe! You are making me tired now. You're like a donkey that must be pulled forward one step at a time. What do you mean you don't know?'

More sniffling took place and, in the dark, Taku squeezed his eyes shut with his fingers and sighed a deep sigh that was the decompression of all his pent-up anger and anxiety. He was beginning to think that he didn't really want to hear this story after all. Surely it would be less troublesome to continue in silence, but every time he allowed the silence the smallest chink of space he would feel his anger towards Jameson rise and then he would curse Jameson and curse himself for always being so unwitting and then he would want to hit something or someone.

'I was walking home past Vashiri's compound and Amai Tsitsi called me to her hut.' As if a dry mouth had been blessed with cool water, the boy was suddenly loquacious. Ah well! Taku reigned in his thoughts of murder and paid attention. 'All I remember is that she told me to go and fetch some meat for a feast. She told me to go quickly while it was still fresh. I left her hut and when I woke up I was in here.'

False alarm, Taku thought to himself, the story had looked to be developing well but it had fizzled out almost as soon as feigned flight. But, even as he returned to cursing his luck in being incarcerated with a milksop who didn't even have the decency to tell a good story about the events leading to his being there, a thought was tugging at his memory. Twisting his already tangled hair he muttered to himself, trying to pull the snippet from out of hiding. 'Bright. Bright. Bright – why is this name familiar to me? Madzimure. Bright Madzimu... Oh! Oh!' In one fluid movement Taku was up, pressed flat against the door as if he could spirit himself through the wood simply by dint of will and banging on it for all he was worth.

'Amaiwe-e zvangu! Officer! Officer! S. O. S., Officer, I beg you! You have locked me in here with a witch's errand boy – must I die like this tonight? Officer, please!' He felt no pain as his fists pounded on the unyielding wood.

'Heeeeeeee!' Taku wailed, at last running out of coherence and giving in to the abject horror of the moment.

The rustling of clothes somehow penetrated Taku's banshee cries and alerted him to the shuffling movements of a body approaching. Taku adopted a fighting stance.

'Stay where you are! Don't come near me. I have coarse salt... see? I know you can't see but I'm spreading it around me. I'm protected. I'll not be any witch's dinner tonight,' he bluffed.

The response was plaintive. 'I won't hurt you. Can't you see, it wasn't me.'

Taku was unmoved. 'I don't care, you still bit off the nose of a dead man. What if your witch mistress comes to visit you tonight and tells you to kill me. I'll not die tonight.' In spite of his fear, or perhaps because of it, Taku was defiant, but the wailing overcame him and rendered him tearful. 'Please God! Heeeeeeee!'

'You can't touch me! I'll not sleep tonight! I'll see you coming.' Taku made himself as small as he could, in the corner in which he now found himself, and continued his lament, 'Oh Kule! Kule, your grandson is in trouble this night.'

*

Papa Sikala shifted restlessly on his reed mat and muttered angrily to himself, '... more trouble than help! Aiiie! My poor bones. This floor is so hard. I could be in my bedroom by now if that boy had come back with my slippers.' Only the crickets responded loudly from somewhere outside. Papa Sikala continued to moan and mutter and was startled out of his morose medley by a loud knocking at the door.

'Who is there at this time of night?' he called out cautiously.

'It's me, Sikala, MaKhumalo. I saw the light from your cooking fire. Why are you sleeping in there?'

'MaKhumalo? What are you doing out at this time of the night?'

'I went to see my daughter in Mutoko and our bus had an accident coming back. The next bus came very late. I'm tired and my bag is too heavy… eh! Sikala, why am I talking through walls? Open the door for me. I'm thirsty and I need to put this bag down, I will fetch it in the morning.'

Sitting up on his mat, Papa Sikala ran many thoughts through his mind as he tried to find the right response.

'Hau! Sikala! Open the door! It's late and I'm tired. I want to go home.'

'So go home. I'm not stopping you.'

'Ko? What has gotten into you, Sikala, that you don't hear what I'm saying? I want to leave this bag with you.'

'How do I know you are really MaKhumalo? This is not the time for decent people to be moving about.'

'Eh eh! Sikala, are you losing your mind? If I am not MaKhumalo then who might I be? Suddenly today you don't know me?'

'Woman, this is the time for witches and their familiars to move about taking people in their sleep and using them as donkeys to carry out their business. You think I'm a foolish old man and you can trick me.'

'A witch! Me?' On the other side of the wall MaKhumalo laughed. To Papa Sikala, the sound was sinister indeed. 'For sure, Sikala, you're a foolish old man. Just open this door and let me be on my way.'

Papa Sikala wished Taku was there and cursed him under his breath again for being so unreliable. At the same time he struggled to find an answer to his dilemma and, coming up with nothing, he remained silent and hoped the voice on the other side would give up and go away.

'Ey wena! Just look through the window and you'll see that it's me.'

172

'Eeeeee! Now you want to steal my eyes. I'm too old to be looking into the faces of witches. I'm old, let me die in peace.'

'Baba wami! Why do you talk such rubbish? Very well, I shall leave my bag by your door. I will come tomorrow for it. I'm too tired to stand here being foolish all night.'

Papa Sikala heaved a sigh of relief and fell back onto his mat determined to stay alert for any more attempts to bewitch him, but before he could say the second line of his prayer, he was deep in sleep, exhausted by the fear and panic that had run through him at the sound of MaKhumalo's voice floating in through the air holes of his hut.

The crowing of his rooster awakened him to a bright new morning. Picking up where he left off, Papa Sikala said his morning prayers in a low voice. Then, slowly pulling the creaking door open, he peeped outside. There was still no sign of Taku. Outside the hens were clucking in the yard and somewhere a dog barked. Papa Sikala wondered how he would get to his field that morning if Taku did not return.

'Empty heads only know how to find trouble! I am sure he bumped into that worthless friend of his – troublemaker!'

As he turned to shut his door and start to see about his breakfast, Papa Sikala heard the creaking of a wheelbarrow. He turned to see a woman walking through the open space in front of his cooking hut.

'Salibonani, scared old man. It's not a witch or a ghost who approaches but MaKhumalo. Do you remember me?'

'MaKhumalo. Oh, I am happy to see you. That boy Taku went yesterday and hasn't come back. Where will I go without shoes? Young people are so cruel.'

'I don't have time for your stories, Sikala, when you can't even help an old friend in a time of need.'

'What are you talking about, Khumalo?'

'You have already forgotten! Here is my bag here. I left it last night when you wouldn't open your door even to give me a drink of water. Look in my face right now! Look at it properly and tell me that it is the face of a witch.'

'MaKhumalo, have you not heard what is happening in this village? All manner of evil things.'

'I have heard, Sikala, and now I'm wearing these patapatas everywhere I go, being scared and foolish just like you – not knowing your friends from your enemies. Rudiah has put salt all around our house to protect us. What would witches want with old fools like you and me?'

'Who knows what goes through their minds. Sending that poor boy to do their work in broad daylight.'

A sudden thought flashed through Papa Sikala's head and he fell silent, watching MaKhumalo through narrowed eyes.

'Eh! Eh! Eh! Eh! Don't you even start your nonsense again. Let me just take my bag and go before you start calling me a witch again.'

'Just wait, Khumalo, bring your wheelbarrow a little closer. Before you go, just take me to my bedroom, I need to get something there.'

'Ho hooooo! Now you want me to help you! You asking a witch to help you? Are you not afraid that I will carry you away and bewitch you?'

'Why would you be a witch today when I have known you all my life? You are the one being foolish now.' Papa Sikala laughed coaxingly. 'I'm not heavy. I'm just a skinny old man and I will be quick. Just come to the stoep here and drop me on my bedroom stoep. You won't even feel the time pass while you wait.'

The sound of MaKhumalo kissing her teeth signalled her reluctant agreement. 'Don't know why I should help you. Making a fragile old woman like me carry you about. Get in, old man, while I'm still standing here like a fool,' she grumbled.

Waiting outside his bedroom, MaKhumalo heard the thud of cupboard doors being shut carelessly, the soft shoop shoop of Papa Sikala's bare feet on the smooth cement floor. After a few minutes she called out.

'What are you still doing in there? Do you think I have nothing better to do than wait on your stoep? I'm getting old standing here.'

Papa Sikala emerged in the open doorway. 'You are already old, Khumalo,' he cackled. 'You and me, Khumalo, but we are made of steel, we don't break easily. We will die standing.' At this he laughed out loud, feeling much braver and happier in the bright light of a new day.

'So you make me stand here and wait for you to get what? Snuff? Where is that boy you live with anyway?'

174

'I wish I knew, Khumalo, but, when I see him, I will be ready for him with a big stick.'

'Just get in. I want to go now, you are beginning to annoy me.'

Papa Sikala, full of renewed good humour, laughed out loud and manoeuvred himself into the wheelbarrow. Leaning back, he smiled charmingly up at MaKhumalo as she hefted the wheelbarrow into a turn.

'Eh Khumalo?' he said in a low voice, motioning for her to lean down as if afraid they would be overheard.

'What is it now?'

'Can we just stop by the toilet. I won't take a minute. You won't even–'

'Eh! Eh! Eh! Sikala. I'm a decent woman, have some respect for me. Do you think I want to wait outside your toilet and listen to your farts. This is your business, you deal with it. Just walk to the toilet yourself, nothing will happen to you.'

'Then give me your shoes if you are not afraid.'

'I'm not afraid but I'm not stupid either, brush your footsteps away with leaves.'

'What if I miss one?'

'Papa wami!'

MaKhumalo, possessed of strength that comes with exasperation, heaved and pushed and, with no ceremony at all, tipped Papa Sikala back onto the stoep of his cooking hut.

'Here you are! Right where I found you. I'm going.'

'Eeee! Khumalo, you are–'

'Don't say anything more. Don't speak to me anymore. Just like a witch, I'm going to disappear in front of your very eyes. Poof! I'm gone.' And with that, she hauled her bag into the wheelbarrow, turned sharply and stalked away with a flap flap flap of her sunset orange patapatas.

Sitting on his stoep, feet safely inside, Papa Sikala watched the day grow tired and begin to fade. He looked up at the sound of panting and watched as a skinny brown dog slunk into his yard.

'Hewo kutu. Where are you coming from looking so tired of life? I'm tired. Tired of waiting for a pair of shoes I don't want.' He sighed deeply, but the dog hunkered down on his front legs and began to growl

175

low in his throat. Incensed, Papa Sikala spoke sternly. 'Don't growl at me in my own yard, dog! I don't even know you.'

The dog only growled louder and began to bark. The chickens scratching in the yard scattered.

'Oh I see! You're hungry and you think you can come and eat my chickens. Well, you just get away from here. Go on!' Leaning out, Papa Sikala picked up a small pebble and threw it at a metal bucket outside his bedroom, but instead of scaring the dog, the sound seemed to make him more menacing.

'Get away from here you four-legged thief! Voetsak!'

Challenged, the dog leapt forward and came towards the open doorway at a run. Forgetting his advanced years and aching body, Papa Sikala leapt up with the agility of a much younger man and slammed the door. Trembling, he leaned against it as the dog continued to growl and bark outside. The sound of distressed chickens flapping and screeching outside taunted him until suddenly the dog yelped and began to whine, the sound growing further and further away.

There was a knock on the door.

'Kule, it's me, Taku, open the door.'

Slowly Papa Sikala peeled himself away from the varnished wood finish of his kitchen door and pulled it open.

'Taku,' his voice was slow and shaky. 'Taaaaaaaku!' he gained in volume and the anger began to build.

'Takundamasimba-asatani Sikala! You were put on this earth to try me. Mambara!' He was shouting now.

'Kule, please. I'm sorry.' Taku receded a couple of steps fearing his grandfather's wrath. He was known to have a quick arm, and a sharp slap around the head was not unknown to Taku. However, Papa Sikala settled into his tirade without any imminent threat of physical violence.

'Leaving an old man defenceless to the mercies of what witch may come and, now, to have my chickens eaten by some mannerless dog because I cannot step outside for a big stick, pissing in a bottle all night, at the mercy of troublesome old women who knock on doors in the middle of the night, God help me, Taku, if I could I would throw you away. What use are you to me?'

'Kule, I am sorry. It was Jam'son's fault. You know how he is, always causing trouble and leaving others to take the blame but you will not envy me the night I had, Kule it wa–'

176

'Jem'son! I didn't send you out to play with Jem'son! I told you I don't want you hanging around with that filthy, no-good son of Washi... you... you...' As if suddenly running out of breath, Papa Sikala stopped. For a moment there was only the sound of laboured breathing. Then, taking a deep breath he straightened.

'Taku! Taku! My grandson. I am old and this body is tired and to be tried like this... '

Grating the legs of a stool across the floor he pulled it to him and sat down abruptly.

'To be undone at this time of my life. To fear the unseen, the unknown. How have I made it this far anyway, in the middle of all this madness, here I stand? Why should I be afraid now?'

Taku had no answer. He stood quietly halfway into the kitchen, plastic bag from Munshanga General Trading in his hands. With a soft grunt and shuffle, Papa Sikala pulled himself up and began to walk out of his kitchen.

'Kule, where are you going?'

Papa Sikala stood outside in the warm soft silt of his front yard and burrowed his toes into the soft sand. He turned to face his grandson and with a peaceful smile on his weathered face he said, 'To my field, on these two calloused feet of mine. I will not be intimidated into erasing my footprints upon this earth. I should not have been afraid, forgetting what I know.'

'What is that, Kule?'

'Shoes are made by man but my feet were made by God – there is nothing to fear in the hand of God.'

Contributors

Raisedon Baya is a leading playwright, theatre director and festival manager based in Bulawayo. He has published a novel, *Mountain of Silence*, an anthology of plays, *Tomorrow's People*, and features in an anthology of folktales, *Around The Fire – Folktales from Zimbabwe*. Some of his stories appear in *Short Writings from Bulawayo II* and *III*, and *Where to Now? Short Stories from Zimbabwe*.

A former teacher and National Arts Council employee who worked at ZBCtv as a producer and commissioning editor, he has written over a dozen critically acclaimed and award-winning plays for television and stage. Several of his plays have toured Africa and Europe.

Two of his plays, *Super Patriots & Morons* and *The Crocodile of Zambezi*, are banned in Zimbabwe. In 2009 Raisedon Baya was a recipient of the Oxfam Novib/PEN Award for Freedom of Expression. He writes a weekly arts column for *The Sunday News*.

Patricia Brickhill is mother to many, enemy to some. Warm-hearted. Likes to laugh. Likes to cry. Makes nice cheesecake. Doppelgänger of 'Adventurer Tree Trunks'.

Murenga Joseph Chikowero has published short fiction in *Storytime* and *Where to Now? Short Stories from Zimbabwe*. He is a graduate of the University of Zimbabwe and the University of Wisconsin-Madison, where he holds a fellowship in the International Division.

Gamu Chamisa is a Zimbabwean writer who lives in Melbourne, Australia. The idea of home and the telling of history inspire her endlessly. She is learning, always. One of her short stories appears in the 2016 Short Story Day Africa anthology, *Migrations*, and she is currently working on more.

John Eppel, born in South Africa in 1947, was raised and still lives in Zimbabwe. His first novel, *D G G Berry's The Great North Road*, won the M-Net prize and was listed in the *Weekly Mail & Guardian* as one of the best 20 South African books in English published between 1948 and 1994. His second novel, *Hatchings*, was short-listed for the M-Net prize and was chosen for the series in the *Times Literary Supplement* of the most significant books to have come out of Africa. His other novels are *The Giraffe Man, The Curse of the Ripe Tomato, The Holy Innocents, Absent: The English Teacher* and *Traffickings*.

His poetry collections include *Spoils of War*, which won the Ingrid Jonker prize, *Sonata for Matabeleland, Selected Poems: 1965 – 1995, Songs My Country Taught Me,* and *Landlocked: New and Selected Poems from Zimbabwe*. He has collaborated with Philani Amadeus Nyoni in *Hewn From* Rock, and with Togara Muzanenhamo in *Textures,* which won the 2015 NAMA Award. He has published three collections of poetry and short stories: *The Caruso of Colleen Bawn, White Man Crawling*, and, with the late Julius Chingono, *Together*.

Eppel's short stories and poems have appeared in many anthologies, journals and websites, including six poems in the *Penguin Anthology of South African Poetry*.

Adrian Fairbairn is a born and raised Zimbabwean who has recently completed a crime thriller novel under the tutelage of renowned South African crime writer Mike Nicol and has now turned his hand to short story writing. A recent winning entrant in a UK publisher's short story competition, his story to be published in a Little Acorn's short story anthology.

T.L. Huchu's fiction has appeared in *Interzone, Space and Time Magazine, Ellery Queen Mystery Magazine, One Throne Magazine, Shattered Prism, Electric Spec, Kasma Magazine, Shotgun Honey, Thuglit, Mysterical-E,* and the anthologies *AfroSF, African Monsters* and *The Year's Best Crime and Mystery Stories 2016*. Between projects, he translates fiction between the Shona and English languages. He is not to be confused with his evil twin @TendaiHuchu, or on www.tendaihuchu.com, whose latest novel *The Maestro, The Magistrate & The Mathematician* was published by amaBooks,

Parthian Press, University of Ohio Press, Peter Hammer Verlag and Farafina.

Donna Kirstein is a poet, writer and creative professional, who grew up in Zimbabwe. Her debut poetry collection *Borderlands* was published by Liquorice Fish in 2017, and her poems and short stories have been included in several anthologies in both the UK and Zimbabwe. Donna currently lives by the seaside in the UK where she works as a graphic designer, photographer and copywriter during the day, and as a writer and artist in the evenings.

Bongani Kona is a Zimbabwean-born writer and editor based in Cape Town. He was shortlisted for the 2016 Caine Prize for African Writing and he is the co-editor of *Migrations*, an anthology of short fiction from Short Story Day Africa. His writing has appeared in numerous publications and websites and most recently in *Safe House*, an anthology of narrative nonfiction from Africa.

Christopher 'Voice' Kudyahakudadirwe is a freelance writer, poet and teacher living and working in South Africa. He holds a Masters of Arts and Creative Writing from the University of the Western Cape. His stories have been published in *Ghost-Eater and Other Stories*. Another of his short stories, 'Voices of the Ancestors', was published in *New Contrast*, one of South Africa's oldest literary magazines. Two of his poems were recently published in *Best 'New' African Poets 2015 Anthology*. Eight of his other poems have appeared in *Harvest: The University of the Western Cape Masters in Creative Writing Poetry Anthology 2016*. His novel, *Murmurings from the Anthill,* is currently with publishers.

Ignatius Mabasa is an award-winning Zimbabwean creative writer, content creator, storyteller, translator and language activist who is an authority in the Shona language and culture. Ignatius started telling stories before he could write his name.
Ignatius studied Shona and Linguistics at the University of Zimbabwe. He received an M.Phil. in Media, Democracy and Development from the University of Oslo in 1998, and, the following year, a Fulbright Scholarship to teach creative writing and Zimbabwean literature in

English in the USA. In 2010, Mabasa was writer/storyteller in residence at the University of Manitoba in Canada.

For 10 years until March 2013, Mabasa worked as Deputy Director of British Council in Zimbabwe and was responsible for all British Council arts and culture programmes.

Currently, he is working on a project to animate folktales and, in the process, promote and preserve an art which plays a key role in the lives of Africans.

Barbara Mhangami-Ruwende is a scholar practitioner in public health, with a focus on minority women's sexual and reproductive health, and founder/director of the Africa Research Foundation for the Safety of Women. She holds degrees from University of Glasgow, Walden University and attended Johns Hopkins Bloomberg School of Public Health. Barbara is a vocal activist and advocate on issues to do with gender-based violence, economic justice for women and gender parity in government institutions.

Her stories and other writings have appeared in *Where to Now? Short Stories from Zimbabwe*, *Still*, the *Journal of African Writing*, *African Roar*, *The Gonjon Pin and Other Stories* and *Guernica Magazine*, as well as on *Storytime* online literary journal and on *Her Zimbabwe*. Her poetry has been published in *Muse for Women* and *African Drum*. She was a 2014 Hedgebrook Writer in Residence and a Caine Prize for African Writing workshop attendee. She is a mentor with the Writivism programme at the Centre for African Excellence (CACE) Foundation and a member of Rotary International.

Christopher Mlalazi is the author of the three novels *Many Rivers*, *Running With Mother*, which has been translated into German and Italian, and *They Are Coming*, and the short story collection *Dancing With Life: Tales from the Township*, which won the Best First Book award at the National Arts Merit Awards and was awarded an Honourable Mention at the NOMA Awards for African Publishing. To date Mlalazi has written and has had staged in Zimbabwe eight plays, including the co-written 2008 Oxfam/Novib PEN Freedom of Expression Award winner *The Crocodile Of Zambezi* and *Election Day*, the National Arts Merit Award winner for Outstanding Theatrical Production in 2010 in Zimbabwe. His poems and short stories are online and in print, including in the Caine Prize's anthology *The Obituary Tango* and *The Literary Review*. He is a former alumnus of the Caine Prize Workshop, Iowa Writers Program, Nordik-Africa Institute and the Hannah-Ardent Scholarship. He is currently writing a new novel, *Blade Maker*, and studying Computer Science.

Mzana Mthimkhulu was born on Martin Luther King's twenty-fifth birthday and was educated at Matshayisikhova and Kuredza Primaries, Inyathi Secondary, Edinburgh College and the then Polytechnic of North London. His short stories and poems have appeared in anthologies, newspapers and magazines in Southern Africa, United Kingdom and online. An enthusiastic culture activist, Mzana is also a newspaper columnist and a playwright.
In 2016 he stunned members of his extended family and his friends when he announced that he had finally completed writing the novel he had spoken about for years.
Mzana and his wife Naume have three biological children and several other traditional ones.

Blessing Musariri has published four children's titles, two of which have won national awards. She writes short stories and poems, which are published in various international anthologies and online magazines. Some of her short stories are published in South African English text books for high schools and have been translated for online magazines. Blessing trained to be a lawyer but her prolific and overactive imagination took over after being called to the English Bar in 1997, and lead her to a more varied, fulfilling life in the world of arts and culture. She holds a Masters degree in Diplomatic Studies (with distinction) from the University of Westminster. Over the years, Blessing has worked as a freelance editing and proofreading consultant, an English teacher and a project co-ordinator for the British Council Harare.

Togara Muzanenhamo was born in Lusaka, Zambia and brought up in Norton, Zimbabwe. He studied Business Administration in Paris and The Hague. He then returned to Zimbabwe and worked as a journalist before moving to an organization dedicated to the development of scriptwriters. In 2001 Muzanenhamo travelled to the United Kingdom to focus on writing poetry. Since then his poems have appeared widely in international journals and magazines. His first collection, *Spirit Brides*, was published by Carcanet Press in 2006 and shortlisted for the Jerwood Aldeburgh First Collection Prize. Togara Muzanenhamo has published two other collections of poems, *Gumiguru,* which was shortlisted for the Glenna Luschei Prize for African Poetry, and *Textures,* poems by John Eppel and Togara Muzanenhamo, which won the National Arts Merit Award for Literature. 'The Silt Path' was commissioned by BBC Radio 4 as part of their *Grounded* series aired in the autumn of 2014.

Melissa Tandiwe Myambo is an author, academic and aerobics instructor, whose story 'La Salle de Départ' was shortlisted for the 2012 Caine Prize for African Writing. Her other writings can be found through her website www.homosumhumani.com. She is the recipient of a 2017 Writing Fellowship at the Johannesburg Institute for Advanced Study and a Fulbright-Nehru Academic and Professional Excellence Research Award to conduct research in India. 'North-South Jet Lag' is part of a collection of short fiction entitled *Airport Stories*.

Thabisani Ndlovu is a senior lecturer of English and Cultural Studies at Walter Sisulu University. Before that, he was Deputy Director and lecturer at the International Human Rights Exchange at the University of the Witwatersrand. His short stories have appeared in various anthologies including *Creatures Great and Small, Short Writings from Bulawayo III, Long Time Coming: Short Writings from Zimbabwe, The Caine Prize for African Writing 2009* and *Where to Now? Short Stories from Zimbabwe.* Other stories have appeared in online journals and magazines. Thabisani has also translated *Where to Now? Short Stories from Zimbabwe* into isiNdebele – *Siqondephi Manje: Indatshana zaseZimbabwe.* In 1992 he won first prize for isiNdebele poetry in the Budding Writers Association National Competition and, in 2005, the inaugural Intwasa koBulawayo Short Story Competition. If he is not writing fiction or poetry, Thabisani carries out humanist-inspired research. If not doing any of those things, he is likely to be thinking about the beautiful and terrible things in life, and trying to find words for them.

Tariro Ndoro holds a Master's degree in Creative Writing from Rhodes University. Her poetry has appeared in numerous literary journals and anthologies including *Kotaz*, *Oxford Poetry* and *New Contrast;* and her fiction has been featured in *AFREADA*.

Bryony Rheam is an author and teacher who lives in Bulawayo with her partner and their two children. She has had nine short stories published in various anthologies and, in 2009, her debut novel, *This September Sun,* was published. It won Best First Book at the Zimbabwe Book Publishers Association Awards in 2010, is a set text for 'A' level Literature in English and, in 2013, it was published in the UK and went to Number 1 as an ebook on Amazon sales.